THE LADY MAYORS OF NORWICH 1923–2017

This book is dedicated to these seventeen remarkable women, whose names will live forever on the magnificent marble slabs within Norwich City Hall

THE LADY LORD MAYORS OF NORWICH 1923–2017

Phyllida Scrivens

PHYLLIDA SCRIVENS

PEN & SWORD HISTORY

First published in Great Britain in 2018
by Pen & Sword History
An imprint of Pen & Sword Books Limited
47 Church Street, Barnsley, South Yorkshire, S70 2AS

Copyright © Phyllida Scrivens 2018

ISBN 978 1 47389 369 6

Typeset in 10.5/13.5 point Palatino by SRJ Info Jnana System Pvt Ltd.

Printed and bound in England by CPI Group (UK) Ltd, Croydon, CR0 4YY

Pen & Sword Books Limited incorporates the imprints of Atlas,
Archaeology, Aviation, Discovery, Family History, Fiction, History, Maritime,
Military, Military Classics, Politics, Select, Transport, True Crime, Air World,
Frontline Publishing, Leo Cooper, Remember When, Seaforth Publishing, The
Praetorian Press, Wharncliffe Local History, Wharncliffe Transport, Wharncliffe
True Crime and White Owl.

For a complete list of Pen & Sword titles please contact

PEN & SWORD BOOKS LIMITED

47 Church Street, Barnsley, South Yorkshire S70 2AS, United Kingdom

email enquiries@pen-and-sword.co.uk

www.pen-and-sword.co.uk

Contents

Illustration Credits

Cover: Norwich City Hall 1951.	With permission from Jonathan Plunkett, George Plunkett's Photographs of old Norwich and Norfolk website.
Cover: Judith Lubbock.	© Archant CM Ltd.
Ethel and Helen Colman.	With permission from Shirley Place.
The original *Hathor*.	With permission from Shirley Place.
Ethel Mary Colman.	With permission from Norfolk Record Office.
Mabel Clarkson at home.	By Lafayette, 26 September 1928, © National Portrait Gallery, London.
Mabel Clarkson at carnival.	Courtesy of East Anglian Film Archive Cat 108, Glimpses of Norwich Carnival 1931.
Joyce Morgan with Margaret Thatcher.	Courtesy of Archant Norfolk.
Joyce Morgan in civic coach.	Courtesy of Archant Norfolk.
Valerie Guttsman outside City Hall.	Courtesy of Archant Norfolk.
Valerie Guttsman in hard hat.	Courtesy of Archant Norfolk.
Barbara Stevenson in car.	Courtesy of Archant Norfolk.
Barbara as child.	With permission from Barbara Stevenson.
Barbara Stevenson family group.	With permission fromAnya Mitchell.
Jill Miller in coach.	Courtesy of Archant Norfolk.
Jill Miller cutting Brian's hair.	Courtesy of Archant Norfolk.
Brenda Ferris portrait.	With permission from Brenda Ferris.
Brenda Ferris and Clint Eastwood.	With permission from Brenda Ferris.

ILLUSTRATION CREDITS

Brenda Ferris outside City Hall.	Courtesy of Archant Norfolk.
Lila Cooper as Dolly Levi.	© Peter King.
Coach in Norvic Drive.	With permission from Alison Bacon.
Robert Climie.	By Bassono Ltd, 10 January 1924, © National Portrait Gallery, London.
Joyce Climie Divers on balcony.	Courtesy of Archant Norfolk.
Felicity Hartley under umbrella.	Courtesy of Archant Norfolk.
Felicity Hartley outside City Hall.	With permission from Felicity Hartley.
Eve Collishaw with portrait.	With permission from Liz Balkwill.
Eve Collishaw with Tim O'Riordan.	© Jeff Taylor, Norwich City Council.
Jenny Lay on her engagement.	With permission from Susie Lay.
Jenny Lay civic group.	© Jeff Taylor, Norwich City Council.
Judith Lubbock in canoe.	With permission from the Broads Authority.
Judith Lubbock inspecting troops.	© Jeff Taylor, Norwich City Council.
Brenda Arthur group at cathedral.	© Jeff Taylor, Norwich City Council.
Brenda Arthur at UEA.	With permission from Brenda Arthur.
Marion Maxwell at Mayor-Making.	© Jeff Taylor, Norwich City Council.
Marion Maxwell at SCVA.	Photo by Andi Sapey, courtesy of Sainsbury Centre for Visual Arts.
Whifflers with Snap the Dragon.	© Jeff Taylor, Norwich City Council.
Sword and Mace Bearers.	© Jeff Taylor, Norwich City Council.
Norwich City Council Chamber.	© Jeff Taylor, Norwich City Council.
The civic coach outside cathedral.	© Jeff Taylor, Norwich City Council.
Past Lord Mayor's badge.	Image reproduced with permission from Norwich City Council.
Motifs from new Lord Mayor's chain.	© Jeff Taylor, Norwich City Council.

Foreword

by Baroness Hollis of Heigham

Norwich has long been a radical city, celebrating the French Revolution (with a maypole), offering safe space to chartists, nonconformists, and refugees from the County and the Continent; and proud of its eminent women, drawn from leading liberal Norwich families and prominent in nineteenth-century progressive causes – anti-slavery and women's suffrage. They sustained city charities, for the frail, the damaged, and the homeless – leaving the impersonal work of contracts and construction to their men.

Norwich's first woman councillor, the university educated Mabel Clarkson, elected in 1913 (Lord Mayor 1930), had insisted that 'the best wealth of a city is in the health of its citizens', demanding free school meals for needy children, a living wage, and decent pensions. She was amongst the first cluster of women councillors nationwide. The wealthy Ethel Colman (1923–24) was the first woman Lord Mayor in the entire country; like Mabel Clarkson, she joined the Labour Party after the First World War. Dorothy Jewson was one of the earliest Labour women MPs. The city regularly had a higher proportion of elected women than most other councils.

In return, women councillors gave the city much – often their life's work – as this engaging, richly detailed, and very readable account of Norwich's seventeen Lady Lord Mayors shows. All but Ethel Colman were elected city councillors. Some senior women had significant committee responsibility: Joyce Morgan for health; Valerie Guttsman for welfare; and Ethel Colman, with her sister, restored and donated Suckling and Stuart halls to the city in 1925. A later woman Lord Mayor, Brenda Ferris, resolutely (and effectively) championed the Arts, and helped turn the halls into Cinema City, and Brenda Arthur, the wise city leader, spent her final year on the Council as Lord Mayor.

Other women had quietly served as conscientious representatives of their wards – the warm Jill Miller, and the gentle Jennie Lay, speaking up for those without a voice. Some women lobbied to be Lord Mayor, this being the height of their ambition; others were surprised and delighted to be offered it. All were profoundly aware that as the city's First Citizen, they inherited centuries of ceremony and dignity, their names joining mayors dating back to 1403 on City Hall's marble wall. In the 1980s, some councillors thought it more 'democratic' to have a chair(man) instead. When pressed whether, on Christmas Day, hospital patients would prefer a visit from the Lord Mayor or a council chair(man), the proposal evaporated.

They worked hard – undertaking up to 800 engagements in the year, up to six a day – though often dismaying their Deputy Lord Mayor and Sheriff, who would have welcomed more engagements than they got. They graced an annual round of receptions and dinners, cathedral services and hospital visits, university graduations and school debates, and voluntary organisations' AGMs, and visited luncheon clubs, fetes, and old people's homes. They welcomed numerous foreign visitors and conference dignitaries to Norwich. Highlights included Royal visits, Royal Garden Parties, twinning events with Rouen, Koblenz or Novi Sad, and always the Lord Mayor's Procession in July, with its floats and bands, raising thousands for her chosen charity. They sought to put their year to good use and good causes. They loved every minute of it.

Several Lord Mayors said afterwards that they had believed they knew the city well, but came to realise how much more texture and richness there was to Norwich: their year had taken them into the quiet corners of civic life, tiny charities, difficult causes, struggling projects and committed volunteers hitherto unknown to them. The press reports that accompanied mayoral visits gave them profile, and often income.

Mayoral years shared a similar rhythm. Mayoral backgrounds were remarkably diverse. Ruth Hardy, a pupil teacher, was the daughter of a warrener (rabbit catcher). Jill Miller, a popular hairdresser, baked her own sausage rolls for receptions. The gutsy USDAW official, Barbara Stevenson, as a backbencher, knitted her way through council meetings, the needles clicking faster as tempers rose. Joyce Morgan, a shop supervisor, and Marion Maxwell, a civil servant trade unionist, both left school at fourteen. Valerie Guttsman was a motherly Czech refugee (her family died in the camps) and a social worker. Brenda Ferris, with roots deep in Norwich, was a translator. Felicity Hartley endured so much bereavement. Her Down's syndrome son became her proud escort. Joyce Divers, a single mother, had to combine mayoralty with part-time work. Judith Lubbock, a teacher, won plaudits for her planning expertise. Jessie Griffiths, a former local government officer, became the first female opposition party leader, hassling Leader Arthur

South (to his amusement). Brenda Arthur, a scientist, but like others deeply experienced in charitable work, headed Age Concern Norwich, before becoming Council Leader.

Always, they were determined never to let the city down. They spent money, which some could ill afford, on suitable clothes for themselves and their escorts (working-class husbands might need new suits, a dinner jacket) although the city helped out with a modest allowance. Women in paid work lost wages. Joyce Morgan acquired twenty evening dresses in her year, courtesy of her employer, whereas Ruth Hardy said she relied on one good black suit. They all struggled with the heavy robes and the heavy (and beautiful) seventeenth-century gold chain that weighed them down.

So many had poor health and stressful private lives. Lila Cooper sadly developed dementia during her year. Others such as the much-loved Jenny Lay, with a working life in social care, and the gallant Marion Maxwell, both debilitated by cancer, discretely managed their health around their civic duties. Marion's speech at City College graduation drew unprecedented applause from its students. With the unobtrusive and unfailing support of civic staff, they performed with courage and grace.

By holding office for just a year, maybe from a minority party, aloof from council politics, confined by ceremony, they had chosen the robes of power rather than power itself. Within such limitations, these 'Lady Lord Mayors' did the city proud, and we are deeply proud of them. They deserve to be remembered.

Patricia Hollis

Patricia Hollis was a Norwich city councillor from 1968–90, serving as Leader for five years from 1983, working closely with a number of former and future Lady Lord Mayors. In 1990 she took the title Baroness Hollis of Heigham, joining the House of Lords as a Labour Peer. Her publications include *Ladies Elect: Women in English Local Government 1865–1914* (Clarendon Press, Oxford, 1987) and the award-winning biography *Jennie Lee: A Life* (Faber & Faber, London, 1997).

Introduction and Acknowledgements

Norwich has had a mayor for over 600 years and the dignity of Lord Mayor was added in 1910, so the office is a good deal older than that of Lord Lieutenant, created by Henry VIII. My father Charles was made Lord Mayor of Norwich in 1965, my grandfather Percy in 1934 and his uncle, Richard, in 1917. I was brought up to appreciate the importance of the office in representing the great City of Norwich. Since I became Lord Lieutenant of Norfolk in 2004, I have got to know twelve holders of the office who have served during that time, seven of whom have been female. They are all rightly proud of their appointments, and fully committed to their civic and charitable duties. It has been a privilege to know them.

(Richard Jewson, Lord Lieutenant of Norfolk, writing in 2017)

If you were to read the names of the mayors and Lord Mayors of Norwich, as chiselled into the Italian marble slabs at the rear of City Hall lobby, you would have to wait over five centuries before reaching the name of a woman. The first Mayor of Norwich, William Appleyard, a wealthy merchant, dates from 1403, and the illustrious list includes the names of influential Norfolk dynasties including Bignold, Bullard, Gurney, Jewson and, of course, Colman. Out of the hundreds of men, as at 2017, there have only been seventeen women entitled to wear the mayoral chain of office. This may not seem many, but by comparison to other cities in this respect, Norwich continues to lead the way. During the same time period, Plymouth has had seven, Bristol nine, Portsmouth ten, Manchester twelve and Stoke-on-Trent fourteen.

The idea for this group biography came to me in May 2012 while interviewing former Lord Mayor Joyce Morgan for my first biography, *Escaping Hitler: A Jewish Boy's Quest for Freedom and his Future.* Joe Stirling, the 'Jewish boy', had served with Joyce as Sheriff of Norwich in the civic year 1975–76. I found Joyce to be warm and welcoming, with a quick sense of humour. As I left she asked: 'Do you think you could write my life story?' I was nonplussed; I had still to finish my first book. Six months later, Joyce died. But I often thought about her request and I hope that, in some small way, I have now fulfilled her wish. Four years later, with the book well under way, I was informed that Past Lord Mayor and Sheriff badges, as presented to former civic Jessie Griffiths, would shortly be sold at an Ipswich auction house. I knew I had to buy them. A month later, I was the proud owner of these beautiful artefacts. I hope that Jessie would have approved of my impulsive action.

Fortunately for me, the surviving nine former Lady Lord Mayors remain living in Norwich. Over eighteen months, I met with each of them, when they shared memories of childhood, careers, family, local politics and their year as Lord Mayor. I am grateful and indebted to Brenda Arthur, Evelyn Collishaw, Brenda Ferris, Felicity Hartley, Judith Lubbock, Marion Maxwell, Jill Miller, Joyce Pitty and Barbara Stevenson.

I located family members, friends and former colleagues to learn more about this group of diverse and remarkable women. I was fortunate to be loaned invaluable photo albums, scrapbooks and shoeboxes filled with letters, telegrams, newspaper cuttings, menus, and gilt-edged invitations. I spent time in the Archant Archives looking at ancient newspapers, and uncovered unpublished memoirs in the research room of Norfolk Record Office. I would like to thank Rosemary Dixon, Sam Earl, Kevin Fitzmaurice, Raymond Frostick, Clare Frostick, Janet Guttsman, Gail Harris, Elvie Herd, Chris Higgins, Glynis Higgins, Patricia Hollis, Vic Hopes, Richard Jewson, Susie Lay, Stephen Lay, Malcolm Martins, Joe Mason, Frank Meeres, Denise Morgan, Sandra Morgan, Rory Quinn, Wendy Quinn, Christopher Seelhoff, Anya Stevenson, Joe Stirling, Christine Sutherland, Jeff Taylor, Gavin Thorpe, Selina Tobin, Doug Underwood, Sandra Underwood, Judith Virgo, Alan Waters and Nick Williams. I also gratefully acknowledge the invaluable financial support provided by the Harry Watson Bursary.

My thanks go to both Baroness Hollis of Heigham for her foreword and the Lord Lieutenant of Norfolk, Richard Jewson, for his personal contribution. In conclusion, I am grateful to my husband Victor and other family and friends, who have been patient and supportive, as I, yet again, indulged my infatuation with the life stories of others.

Phyllida Scrivens, Norwich, June 2017

Map of the most recent sixteen Norwich City Council ward boundaries, as at 2004. Mancroft Ward represents the centre of the city. Although there have been many boundary changes over the decades, this gives an approximation of where each of the Lady Lord Mayors held her council seat.

CHAPTER 1

Ethel Mary Colman (1863–1948)

Lord Mayor of Norwich 1926–27

The latest month they had her (*Hathor*) out was November. 'I can remember,' relates our Lord Mayor, 'waking one morning at Buckenham in the Horse Shoes Reach on November 9th (Lord Mayor's Day) to a scene of surpassing beauty. Turning to our log book I find I made the following entry: "Wednesday, November 9th, 1910. When we looked out in the morning we found everything covered with a rime frost and looking most beautiful. We sailed as far as Cantley, turning just above the Red House, and then sailed back to Brundall."' 'I little thought then,' said Miss Colman, 'that exactly thirteen years later I should be donning the Lord Mayor's robe and chain myself!'

(*Eastern Daily Press*, November 1926)

As Ethel Colman was escorted into the Council Chamber at Norwich Guildhall[1] on 9 November 1923, she was greeted with hearty cheers. It was the first time that anyone had seen the distinctive black and gold civic robes draped over a female form.

When it was initially proposed that she become the first female Lord Mayor of Norwich, and indeed the first in Great Britain, she politely declined, fearing that the work and responsibilities might be too great for her. Ethel certainly had excellent credentials. During the second half of the nineteenth century, her great-great-uncle, Jeremiah Colman, her

1

father, Jeremiah James Colman, and her older brother Russell had all served as Sheriff and Mayor of Norwich. Her father was also Liberal MP for Norwich from 1871–95, and in 1881 was made Deputy Lieutenant for Norfolk.

Ethel felt obliged to consider the offer seriously, almost certainly taking advice from the family. Why was she hesitating? She supported women's suffrage, strongly believing that women should take a part in public life, and she had considerable experience of presiding over both public and private meetings. She was known for her sound common sense, held no fear of public speaking, had shown level judgment and had a gentle sense of humour. Each of these qualities would stand her in good stead when working alongside councillors, the majority of whom, of course, were men. In addition, the Colman family had been much loved and revered in the city for more than half a century, since the transference of the Colman Mustard Works from its original home in Stoke Holy Cross to Norwich in 1856. That was evident from the response of the public in September 1898, when her father died.

Ethel had never forgotten her father's funeral. The shops had been closed and traffic at a standstill. As the seemingly endless funeral cortège of carriages travelled towards Princes Street Chapel, the streets were lined with people, the women sobbing and men doffing their hats. Behind the hearse came a column of wagons, each loaded high with floral tributes, led by heavy horses whose flanks were adorned with polished brasses on leather straps. Walking behind the carts were over 1,200 employees from Carrow Works. These memories reassured Ethel that she would receive due respect in the Council Chamber as well as the assistance of colleagues when necessary. Foremost in her thoughts was the fact that, had her older sister Laura lived beyond her sixtieth year, it would most certainly have been her that the Aldermen of Norwich would have chosen as Lord Mayor. When they approached Ethel again a few days after she first turned it down, she graciously accepted, in memory of Laura.

Jeremiah James and his wife Caroline had been devoted parents. Ethel Mary, a sister for Laura and Russell, was their third baby in as many years, born into a devout nonconformist Christian family on 12 February 1863. Over the following seven years, the couple had three more children – Helen, Alan and Florence. The Colman heirs were brought up and educated in Carrow House, a gentleman's mansion of neoclassical design, until 1878, when their father bought the much larger and stunningly beautiful Carrow Abbey, a former twelfth-century Benedictine nunnery. It took ten years to restore the building to Jeremiah's satisfaction. Following the move, the family's former home was refurbished, becoming the administration offices for the Carrow Mustard Works.

Once she reached fourteen, Ethel was sent to Clapham Park in London as a boarder at Miss Pipe's School for Young Ladies, joined later by her sister Helen. Headmistress Hannah Pipe, originally from Manchester, was a signatory of the 1866 Women's Suffrage Petition.[2] At least one of her impressionable young ladies would later join the militant arm of the suffragettes.[3] Once permanently back home in Norwich, the sisters resumed their regular worship at Princes Street Congregational Church. They rediscovered their love of country walks and the delights of the Norfolk Broads and rivers, the family chauffeur being always on hand to return them to Carrow Abbey.

The spring and summer of 1890 was an exciting time for the Colman girls, with older sister Laura in the process of arranging her marriage to Professor James Stuart, a Scot from Fifeshire. They had first met James when Laura presented him to her parents during the previous autumn. Jeremiah had been suffering with painful episodes of gout, but his ill temper much improved as he engaged in animated discussion with this Professor of Mechanics and Fellow of Trinity College Cambridge. The wedding took place on 16 July at Princes Street, the Carrow workers raising enough money to buy a diamond bracelet for the bride.

James quickly became an integral part of the Colman family, taking control of the ongoing restoration of Carrow Abbey, whilst encouraging his wife to become a city councillor. Founding the University Extension Movement at Cambridge, he arranged lectures aimed at the cultured middle classes, notably women, many of which were held in Norwich. Ethel was fascinated by the concept of continuing learning, attending the first Norwich event in 1877. Inspired by hearing Mr Wyn Roberts speak about Benedictine buildings in Britain and on the Continent, Ethel became an enthusiastic devotee, and was later elected as President of the Norwich University Extension Society, a role she held for twenty-two years.

The family had much to celebrate in 1893, with youngest brother Alan graduating from Cambridge and Jeremiah being conferred with the Honorary Freedom of the City. However, two years later, Caroline's health began to give cause for concern. She was packed off to the family holiday home, Cliffe House[4] at Corton on the Suffolk coast, in the hope that the sea air would revive her. Caroline was on the road to recovery in April 1895, when her elderly father, William Hardy, suddenly died. Having lost her mother only four years previously, Caroline was consumed with grief; she subsequently died, aged sixty-four, on 5 July, and was laid to rest in the Rosary Cemetery in Norwich.[5] Struggling to cope without the irreplaceable love and support of his dear wife, Jeremiah resigned from his parliamentary seat to spend more time with his family and business.

In June 1896, Alan felt unwell. He too was sent to Corton for rest and recuperation, spending the entire summer there, frequently visited by doctors from Norwich and London who eventually diagnosed tuberculosis. In September, Alan returned to Norwich but the journey brought on a relapse. On 20 November, Laura and Helen accompanied the invalided Alan on the P&O Steamer *Simla*, heading for Egypt and the restorative dry desert heat. A few weeks later, Jeremiah, Ethel and Florence travelled to join them. Unfortunately, Russell was unable to get away. He would never see his little brother again.

Alan's dying wish was to sail on the Nile aboard a traditional *dahabeah*, a barge-like luxury passenger boat with two sails. Jeremiah hired the vessel *Hathor* and the entire party headed for Luxor and the Valley of the Kings. Youngest sister Florence, a keen amateur photographer, kept herself distracted by recording much of the trip, taking more than 300 images. In an autobiographical tribute to her brother, Laura wrote touchingly about his final hours on the boat:

> The evening before he passed away there was a sunset wonderful even among Egyptian sunsets. Looking westward from the *Hathor*, one saw the Nile flowing like a mass of liquid burnished silver. ... When the rich colours had died away, the crescent moon appeared, and the sky seemed pierced with myriads of stars.[6]

Early the next morning, on Sunday, 7 February 1897, Alan quietly passed away. He was thirty years old.

Devastated, the family returned to Norwich, where Alan's remains were interred in his mother's plot. Jeremiah threw himself back into work but suffered from frequent bouts of depression. On a happier family note, youngest daughter Florence was planning a wedding. On 9 September 1898, she would marry architect Edward Boardman.[7] Jeremiah felt too unwell to give her away but he was there to greet the guests for the reception. One week after the wedding, Jeremiah's 93-year-old mother died. Three days later, Jeremiah sank into unconsciousness. Newly-weds Dorothy and Edward were summoned home from their honeymoon at Calthorpe Broad. In his last will and testament, Jeremiah bequeathed to the city major works of arts and an important book collection; to the family, the vast sum of over £687,000, the equivalent of nearly £83m today.[8]

As spinster women, living on their own substantial means, Ethel and Helen were well placed to immerse themselves in philanthropic projects, be they religious, intellectual or social. They extended their keen interest in the welfare of the Colman employees, many of whom lived in the industrial village of Trowse. Developed by the company over five decades, the model village was proving inspirational for both Lord Lever's Port Sunlight and the Cadbury Brothers' village of Bournville. But Ethel's abiding passion was exploring the waterways of the Norfolk Broads. Following Alan's death, she and Helen sought a way to commemorate his life. In October 1904, they commissioned a traditional Norfolk wherry from boatbuilder Daniel Hall of Reedham. They commandeered the artistic skills of Dorothy's husband, Edward, who agreed to decorate the sycamore panels and interior doors, creating delicate and elegant designs inspired by the Egyptian artefacts in the British Museum. In memory of Alan's death on the Nile aboard the original *Hathor*, this new vessel was given the same name and launched on 2 August 1905. The first signatures in the leather-bound visitors' book were those of Edward and Florence. That day, their daughter Joan released a flock of pigeons to mark the occasion.[9]

During the season from May to October, accompanied by only a skipper and a mate, Ethel and Helen regularly sailed on *Hathor*, spending nights away at Reedham, Whitlingham, Brundall, Acle, Horning and Ludham Bridge. They invariably took a walk in the evening air, sometimes as far as 5 miles. *Hathor* was the perfect venue for entertaining extended family, friends and business contacts. In the summer of 1908, they welcomed the celebrated writer H. Rider Haggard, who was living in Ditchingham House near Bungay, and the famous composer Henry J. Wood, who inscribed the visitors' book with a musical score. With their characteristic generosity, the sisters regularly invited groups of staff from Carrow Works, nurses from Norwich hospitals and their own domestic staff to join them for a sail on the Yare. Ethel meticulously recorded each voyage in the logbook, whether or not she had been aboard that day.

Neither James Stuart nor his wife Laura lived to see Ethel become Lord Mayor. James died at his home in Carrow Abbey in October 1913, aged seventy. He was much missed. To honour his memory, in 1915 Ethel and Helen commissioned a block of twenty-two small flats to be built in Recorder Road, rehousing some of those worst affected by the catastrophic Norwich flood of 1912. The development was named Stuart Court. Laura survived her husband by seven years, dying childless at sixty on 4 November 1920. Laura had been a much-loved role model for her younger sisters: the first woman magistrate in Norwich, a city councillor, President of the Norwich Branch of the National Union of Women's Suffrage Societies and the author of their mother's biography.

With the onset of the Great War, the employees of Carrow Works answered the call to arms, with many men joining the Eighth Norfolks (Service) Battalion. Colman's supported the volunteers by offering them additional weekly allowances. Women, out of necessity, were given traditionally male roles, including administrative roles and in the Tin Box Department. *Hathor* was laid up for the duration of the conflict, with Laura, Ethel and Helen devoting their time to alleviating the wartime challenges faced by company workers, both at home and those fighting overseas.

On the last day of October 1923, it was announced that Miss Ethel Mary Colman had consented to become the first lady Lord Mayor of Norwich, and consequently the first in Great Britain. This news was deemed so momentous that it was promptly cabled across the Atlantic, appearing in an American newspaper that same day, *The New York Times* publishing Ethel's photograph a month later on Sunday, 2 December.[10] On her Mayor-Making day, Ethel concluded her acceptance speech with a surprising announcement:

> As to work outside the Council, I will do what I can. I am sorry that I shall not be able to accept invitations to open bazaars. If invitations to public dinners are not accepted, I hope this will not be considered discourteous.[11]

Three years after Laura's death, the sisters acquired the perfect memorial to their late sister when Suckling House, one of the oldest surviving merchant houses in the city, became available. By the early 1920s, the building, originating in the fourteenth century, had fallen into disrepair. Ethel and Helen resolved to carry out renovations, build an extension – to be known as Stuart Hall – and present it as a gift to the city. Once again, Edward led the design team, creating a public hall to hold 450 people, fitting it with modern apparatus including a cinema projector and screen.[12] Ethel and Helen arranged for the official presentation to the City Council to coincide with a visit to Norwich by HRH the Duke of York on 25 October 1925. The family could not have been more proud.

As a music lover, Ethel was particularly pleased that the revival of the Norwich Triennial Music Festival, which had lapsed since the start of the Great War, would take place during her final weeks in office. Ethel became one of the first women to join the prestigious Festival Committee, volunteering the recently renovated Suckling House as the venue for a celebratory luncheon and a tea party, where Norwich elite could meet with members of the new Queen's Hall Orchestra. On 31 October 1924, Queen Mary and her new daughter-in-law, Elizabeth the Duchess of York,[13] arrived in Norwich to be greeted by the Lord Mayor at St Andrew's Hall. On the programme that afternoon was Dr Vaughan Williams conducting his own work, *Sea Symphony*, with Sir Henry Wood as 'guest conductor' for the National Anthem. As the final note died away, someone in the west gallery spontaneously called for three cheers for England's Queen, the Norwich audience complying with enthusiasm.

Ethel witnessed two general elections during her mayoral year, with local girl Dorothy Jewson elected in December 1923 as one of the first female Labour MPs. Less than a year later, Dorothy lost her seat and despite her best efforts, there was to be no return to Westminster. In 1927, she stood for Norwich City Council, the same year that Ethel returned to serve as Deputy Mayor to the city's first Labour Lord Mayor, Herbert Edward Witard. In 1929, Ethel received a further accolade when the hierarchy of Princes Street Congregational Church elected her as a Life Deacon, recognising her lifelong service to her church. Ethel pointed out that six of the eight Liberal Lord Mayors of Norwich had also been nonconformist deacons, adding that it was not a bad record for the churches and the part they play in civic life.[14]

Helen Colman died on 5 July 1947, aged eighty-two, one year after her brother Russell. In many ways, Helen had spent her life supporting her elder, more elevated sibling, while quietly devoting her life to her own philanthropic, educational and literary causes. Without her lifelong companion, Ethel faded, passing away on 23 November 1948. It was left to Florence,[15] as the only surviving sibling, to lead the mourners at Ethel's simple funeral, held not in the grandeur of Norwich Cathedral, but in the Congregational Church in Princes Street.

It was the journalist from the *Eastern Daily Press* who, when Ethel stood down as Lord Mayor, summed up the future of civic appointments: 'If the election of a lady as Lord Mayor were considered an experiment, it has been an unqualified success, and as opportunity occurs will undoubtedly be repeated.'[16]

Endnotes

1. Norwich Guildhall was built in 1407–13, the largest and most elaborate city hall outside London, with its distinctive chequered effect exterior. Over the centuries the building has been extended and refurbished countless times, housing a prison, a courtroom, a police station, a storage place for swords and regalia, the City Corporation Council Chamber, the Sheriff's Parlour, a tourist information centre and a café.

2. The first mass petition for Votes for Women presented to Parliament, with over 1,500 names.

3. Elizabeth Rowe, a contemporary of Ethel, was sentenced in November 1911 to two months in Holloway Prison for smashing the windows of the National Bank near the Strand in London. Crawford, Elizabeth, *The Women's Suffrage Movement: A Reference Guide 1866–1928*, Psychology Press, 2001.

4. Cliffe House has now fallen into the sea.

5. Born into the influential local Cozens-Hardy dynasty, Caroline was central to the family's success and popularity, spearheading the pioneering welfare programme for company workers, encouraging her daughters to teach at the Carrow Men's Day School and Sunday School. She was a loving mother and a lifelong supporter of many Norwich charitable organisations including the Jenny Lind Hospital for Children, Caroline forever grateful to the doctors there for saving the life of her firstborn, Russell, when as an infant he fell dangerously ill.

6. *In Memoriam – Alan Cozens-Hardy Colman*, by his sister, Laura E. Stuart, December 1898.

7. Edward Thomas Boardman, Lord Mayor of Norwich 1905–1906.

8. http://www.bankofengland.co.uk/education/Pages/resources/inflationtools/

9. Amongst the crowd was local child Elizabeth Crossley. Exactly 100 years later, Elizabeth's daughter was invited to Reedham to re-enact the launch.

10. *Carrow Works Magazine*, Vol. XV11, No. 2, January 1924.

11. *Eastern Daily Press*, 10 November 1923.

12. The building was refurbished and opened in April 1978 as Cinema City – see chapter 9.

13. Elizabeth Bowes Lyon married Prince Albert, Duke of York, on 26 April 1923.

14. Rawcliffe, Carole, *Norwich Since 1550*, Hambledon, London, 2004.

15. Florence Boardman lived a further twelve years, dying in July 1960, aged ninety-one.

16. *Eastern Daily Press*, 10 November 1924.

CHAPTER 2

Mabel Maria Clarkson (1875–1950)
Lord Mayor of Norwich 1930–31

I am not going to seek to harrow your feelings, to make a sentimental appeal, but only to put before you two or three instances leading up to my point. My first case concerns the conditions of a man, woman and five children. To get to them you grope your way up two flights of steep, dark stairs, to two rooms. Up those stairs every drop of water has to be carried. It has to be boiled in a saucepan even for the washing of the five children. The walls, rotten and crumbling, look as if a push would send them out, and when damp give out such a smell that disinfectant has to be used freely. In the one bedroom where the seven sleep you have to walk warily or you step into a great hole; the rain and the snow drive in. The man suffers from chronic asthma, and is unlikely to work again. … And so we get unhealthy children crowding our school clinics, growing up into diseased and inefficient men and women, swelling the army of the unemployables, filling our sanatoria.

(Mabel Clarkson, addressing the Norwich Rotary Club, 1930)

Conservative Councillor Frederick Jex[1] was about to propose a woman as Lord Mayor of Norwich, only the second in the history of the city. Although she was in the opposing political party, Fred had no doubts about her ability to perform this senior civic role. Two years previously, in 1928, Miss Clarkson had been elected as the first female Sheriff[2]

9

of the city. Fred also knew of her twenty-five years spent working to improve the living conditions for the more poverty stricken in the city. He warmly commended her appointment.

Having taken the oath and been invested with robes and chain of office, Mabel took centre stage; she was no stranger to public speaking. Using similar rhetoric to that of Ethel Colman in *her* acceptance speech in 1923, Mabel made her intentions perfectly clear:

> Unemployment, housing, slum clearing, education, health, an endless list of duties now laid on municipalities, to my mind must make first demand on the time and energies of the First Citizen. … Certain social functions, including the opening of bazaars and sales, I shall seldom have the pleasure of attending. … If I refuse invitations, believe it is not because I am resting in an armchair in the Lord Mayor's Parlour but engaged in other work.[3]

Although not born in Norfolk, as a young woman she was no stranger to the county. Mabel's father, Richard Clarkson, was born in the North Norfolk village of West Barsham in 1832. Her grandfather was Luke Hall Clarkson, a wealthy retired farmer. Richard trained as a solicitor, marrying Elizabeth Prince, the daughter of a Hereford magistrate, in July 1863. Richard joined a law firm in the market town of Calne in Wiltshire, where his son Charles was born in 1865, followed by four daughters, Mary, Ethel, Ada, and finally, Mabel Maria, arriving on 1 June 1875. Mabel retained few memories of her father, for when she was three years old Richard Clarkson died, aged only forty-six, leaving his widow 'living on her own means'.[4]

In the summer of 1892, Elizabeth and her girls travelled from their home in Reading[5] to East Anglia, to be honoured guests at a very special occasion. The village of Market Weston near Thetford was adorned with flags, flowers and wicker arches, many with banners bearing inscriptions such as 'God Bless the Happy Pair'. Charles Clarkson was marrying Elsie, the second daughter of parish rector the Reverend Edmund Daubeney. Having studied history and theology at Oxford University, Mabel's big brother was now twenty-seven and Rector of Ampton, a village just 10 miles from Market Weston. Residents of both villages were there, cheering and clapping as the guests entered the church, resplendent in their best formal attire. Mabel's elder sisters, Mary and Ethel, were amongst the bridesmaids, dressed in white silk dresses, trimmed with ribbons and ruches of terracotta pink. Elizabeth presented the bride with a pearl ring and a topaz and turquoise necklace.

It was a truly wonderful family occasion, Elizabeth's only sadness being that Richard had not survived to see his son's happiest day.

Charles was installed as Rector of All Saints Church in the Suffolk village of Lawshall[6] in 1899, his wife giving birth to Dorothy on 11 January 1900. With only her two spinster daughters, Ethel and Mabel, still living at home, the three ladies moved to Troston, a village 15 miles distance from her baby granddaughter. By 1904, for reasons that are unclear, Elizabeth, Ethel and Mabel had moved to the city of Norwich, sharing a house at 3 Mile End Road with their cook and housemaid, an arrangement that continued until Elizabeth's death on 17 January 1918.

Mabel explored Norwich on her bicycle, appalled by the sights, smells and sounds of the city's notoriously overcrowded slum dwellings. She immediately applied to join the Norwich Board of Poor Law Guardians and was elected in 1905, successfully lobbying Norwich City Council to offer classes in laundry and cooking to unemployed factory girls to improve their chances of domestic employment.[7] Her life's work had begun.

In November 1913, Mabel stood as a Liberal for a seat on Town Close Ward, an option first extended to women in the Local Government Act of 1894. As she addressed her election rally, Mabel was focused, her voice passionate:

> I believe that the best wealth of a city is in the health of its citizens. I shall always be in favour of feeding children who are in want; giving them a good education; paying the worker a living wage; caring for the sick in the hospitals and asylums, and pensions for aged workers.[8]

Mabel won the seat, becoming the City Council's first woman councillor, a lone but strong female voice amongst the ranks of men. In 1922 she was appointed as one of the first female magistrates, a role she carried out with dignity and compassion. However, at the local elections of early November 1923, Mabel lost her council seat to the Conservative candidate. This may have prevented her being present in the Guildhall later the same month, when Ethel Colman became the first female Lord Mayor of Norwich.

The general election of October 1924 saw the Liberal Party losing the majority of its seats in Parliament, leading Mabel to reconsider her political allegiance. In 1925 she defected to the more progressive Labour Party, later winning a council seat in Heigham Ward. Her decision may have been influenced by the success of Dorothy Jewson,[9] a Norwich girl

11

and nine years Mabel's junior, elected in 1923 as Norwich's first female Member of Parliament, and one of the first four women in the country to be elected as a Labour MP. Mabel would have known of Dorothy's work on poverty in Norwich, most probably scrutinising Dorothy's pamphlet 'The Destitute of Norwich', published in 1912. The two women shared common goals, serving together as Labour councillors from 1927 to 1932, no doubt passionately challenging the Conservative-led administration at every opportunity. Mabel was promoted to Alderman in 1932, the same year that the Labour group first gained control of the Corporation. Throughout her political career Mabel chaired a number of prestigious committees, including Social Welfare, Education and Health. She worked with many charitable organisations,[10] notably for twenty-five years as Chairman of the Norwich School Children's Boot Fund.

Mabel served the city as First Citizen with zeal and energy, never missing a chance to promote her good causes, and sharing her engagements with older sister Ethel as Lady Mayoress. One of Mabel's first duties was to preside over the Armistice Day commemorations. A crowd of almost 20,000 citizens filled the Market Square. With four minutes to go before the traditional two-minute silence, the mace bearers appeared from the Guildhall, followed by a procession with the Lord Mayor, Sheriff Benjamin Morgan, councillors, corporate officials, members of the clergy and ex-servicemen organisations. At exactly 11.00 am, a time signal burst from the castle battlements and the hooter sounded from Caley's chocolate factory. The flags on the Guildhall and the castle dropped to half mast. The silence throughout the city was palpable. A pair of trumpeters from the Light Brigade Royal Artillery sounded the Last Post and Reveille. The town clerk handed the civic wreath to Mabel, who placed it at the base of the memorial outside the Guildhall, before the procession slowly made its way back inside.[11]

Mabel's high profile role provided her with further opportunities to spread her message of compassion. She was certainly on good form at the Lord Mayor's lunch with members of the Norwich Rotary Club, traditionally the first luncheon event held for the new Lord Mayor and Sheriff following their appointment. Having eaten an excellent meal, many may have suffered indigestion as the Lord Mayor described, in graphic detail, the dreadful conditions in which many poorer Norwich residents lived. In conclusion she urged the all-male Rotarians to consider visiting the families, as she had, to witness the unacceptable squalor, pointing out that with their help, enough money might be raised to achieve the complete abolition of the Norwich slums, creating a 'City Beautiful' in their place.[12] Mabel was a visionary, totally focused on improving lives. She rarely diluted her message, her speeches carefully designed to combine wit, self-deprecation, sincerity and hard facts, an effective combination that hit hard and secured results.

Much to everyone's delight, Mabel's name appeared on the King's Birthday Honours list of 2 June 1931, being appointed a Commander of the Order of the British Empire (CBE) for public and political services. She was in good company, with Sir Edward Elgar, Benjamin Rowntree and actress Miss Sybil Thorndike among the other recipients. On arriving to open the Brabazon Society Annual Bazaar a few weeks later, she received many warm words of congratulation. Despite her public pledge not to attend such events, this was an occasion that Mabel was happy to patronise. A forerunner to occupational therapy, the Brabazon scheme was first introduced into a London workhouse in 1882 by Lady Meath, wife of Lord Brabazon, providing a programme of activities for the elderly and infirm, with the aim, as Lady Meath put it, 'to stop their incessant grumbling'.[13] As Mabel opened the sale of work, she admired the display of quilts, rugs, woodcarvings, wrought iron work, lace and painted crockery. She urged patrons to buy everything on the stalls; the money raised would provide treats for the workhouse inmates, including trips out, warm clothes and nourishing food.

Norwich has a tradition of expansive carnival processions and the one held in aid of the Norfolk and Norwich Hospital in July 1931 was no exception. The organiser, Captain Hurt, aimed to raise £1,000 to help ease the deficit of £41,000. The procession began at Newmarket Road at 4.00 pm, accompanied by a marching band. Norwich's Snap the Dragon made an appearance and the highlight was a 40-foot long 'Mingo the Measle', a snakelike contraption propelled by twenty boys from the City of Norwich School. Early in the evening Mabel took up her position on a raised platform outside the hospital entrance, dressed in a loose fitting skirt and jacket, shirt and man's tie, topped with a fashionable bowler-style hat with wide ribbon. As she bent low to present the trophies to the winning floats, she was forced to hold tightly to the mayoral chain, for fear it would hit a prize-winner in the face! But her smile was genuine; it had been a fun day.[14]

Mabel retired from the Aldermanic Bench in 1948 when she was seventy-three. She had become a legend in the city, known to young and old, rich and poor. She had quietly gone about her duty, a philanthropist who asked for no reward, a determined hands-on campaigner. She

13

suffered from ill health during her final two years, dying at her home in Mount Pleasant on 20 March 1950. Her sister Ethel, having lost her soulmate, her lifelong companion and best friend, quietly faded away, dying exactly one month later.

There was one particular event held in February 1931 that must have interested Mabel intently. The Norwich Publicity Association invited her to its annual meeting, where architect Robert Atkinson, a former Director of Education to the Architectural Association, would be giving an address. Using an extraordinary blend of prose and poetry, Atkinson described his observations, drawn during the previous evening as he walked alone around the city, armed only with an ordnance map and a notepad. His opening remarks set the tone:

> I am amused. I am tickled to death. I am to talk to you of Norwich,
> to *you*, who have lived your lives in the city and know it like a book.
> I, a stranger, am to see things in Norwich that you cannot see.

Having effused about the many churches, bridges, medieval merchants' houses and numerous gateways, he concluded his speech with a radical suggestion:

> Everyone is talking of bypass roads and street widening. You have a road to hand; ready-made, the finest possible, and affording an opportunity that is unique. I refer to the old wall enclosing the city. On that wall, in almost every position, are slum dwellings put up during the last fifty years. It would be a great adventure to clear them all out and open up the road following the wall, which has always been a natural highway. Do this, and you will have a wonderful circulating boulevard all around the city and its cost would be comparatively nothing.[15]

It would be thirty years before this prophetic vision would be realised.

Endnotes

1. Fred Jex was born into poverty and worked in the Norwich boot and shoe industry, becoming a full-time official with the National Union of Boot and Shoe Operatives. Elected to the City Council, he became known as 'The Prime Minister of Norwich'. He campaigned vigorously for decent working conditions and improved housing. A number of roads in Norwich are named after him.
2. King Henry IV's charter in 1404 allowed the Freemen of the City to elect

councillors, aldermen, two sheriffs and a mayor, serving for one year. Sheriffs collected taxes on behalf of the monarch and helped the mayor maintain law and order. Changes in national legislation over the centuries means that now the position of Sheriff is ceremonial, serving alongside the Lord Mayor.

3. *Eastern Daily Press*, November 1930.
4. Ancestry.co.uk. Elizabeth Anne Clarkson, 1901, England Census.
5. The Clarkson girls were privately schooled in Reading, Mabel later taking a degree at the university there.
6. Charles was rector in Lawshall until his death in 1923.
7. Hollis, Patricia, *Ladies Elect: Women in English Local Government 1865–1914*, Clarendon Press, Oxford, 1987, p.458.
8. Election address, 1 November 1913, as reproduced in *Ladies Elect*.
9. Dorothy Jewson, 1884–1964.
10. Others included the Norwich District Visiting Association, Norwich Office for the National Council of Women, Norwich and District Nursing Association and the League of Nations Union.
11. *Eastern Daily Press*, 12 November 1930.
12. *Eastern Daily Press*, November 1930.
13. Hollis, Patricia, *Ladies Elect*, p.280–1.
14. *Glimpses of the Norwich Carnival 1931*, amateur film held in East Anglia Film Archive, University of East Anglia.
15. Illustrated pamphlet by the Norwich Publicity Association, June 1931.

CHAPTER 3

Ruth Elsie Hardy
(1890–1975)
Lord Mayor of Norwich 1950–51

Great Aunt Ruth and her sisters did not need Women's Lib to assert their supremacy over men. It simply existed plain for all to see. Ruth was the shortest of the girls, but made up for it by climbing the ladder of local government and the judiciary in Norwich and clearly enjoying every minute. She represented a kind of post-war socialism long dead, values that stood for grants not loans in education, publicly owned council housing and light airy secondary modern schools.

(Andrew Anderson, great-nephew to Ruth Hardy, writing in 2015)

While Phipp Peachey trapped, skinned and stuffed straw into rabbits, his wife Susannah was occupied raising ten children, firstly in Lakenheath in Suffolk, and from 1905 on the Jeremiah James Colman's estate in Bixley, just south of Norwich. Phipp worked as a warrener, harvesting rabbits. There was no spare money for luxuries. Phipp once found himself in trouble with his master when caught selling rabbits to the local butcher. He kept his job, but was no longer allowed to wear the Colman livery – a great ignominy for him. Phipp and Susannah first met in Wandsworth, Surrey, when Phipp worked in a butcher's shop and Susannah in service. They married in All Saints Church, Wandsworth, on 3 June 1883, their first child, Thirza, born two years later. Susannah was a feisty lady, raising her five girls to be independent, forceful and ambitious.

Second daughter Emily became a 'dotty fundamentalist' who fervently disapproved of her own daughter's choice of husband. Beatrice, child number five, developed into 'a mischievous lady who wore pillbox hats and fox fur with glass eyes that glinted menacingly as she pinned you against her chest'.[1] But it was the couple's fourth child, Ruth Elsie, born in January 1890 in Lakenheath, whose destiny it was to don the large black plumed hat of civic office. She would welcome royalty to the city of Norwich and dine in London's Mansion House, alongside the Secretary of State and Archbishop of Canterbury, enjoying Lobster Neuberg and Veuve Clicquot champagne.

The children were educated at the village school in Trowse, later transferring to the Norwich Municipal Secondary School. Ruth's ambitious elder sister Thirza was the first to become a teacher, with Ruth following her example, staying on at the school as a trainee. In 1912 she married local boy Bertie Harry Hardy, and the couple moved into Norwich after the wedding. Bertie, the son of Thomas Hardy, a bricklayer from Trowse working for Colman's Mustard, was three years older than Ruth and already qualified as a teacher. In 1914, with the onset of the Great War, Bertie joined the Royal Army Medical Corps, spending most of his service in France and being promoted to rank of sergeant.

Finding herself alone in Norwich, travelling every day to teach at a school in Cromer, Ruth decided to join the Independent Labour Party, a political party that unusually accepted men and women as equal members and supported the concept of universal suffrage. Ruth was proud to call herself a socialist. At the end of the war Bertie and Ruth were reunited. In September 1920, his French much improved through years spent on the Continent, Bertie joined the staff at the prestigious City of Norwich School for Boys (CNS) in Eaton, as a Master of French. Established by Norwich City Council as a boy's secondary school, CNS awarded scholarships to the most intelligent boys in the city's primary schools. Modest and unassuming, with a gentle sense of humour, over his career Bertie included his two great-nephews amongst his hundreds of students. He remained an academic for thirty-two years, retiring as Deputy Headmaster in 1952.

On 18 August 1922, Marion Ruth Suzette was born. There would be no others. During the 1920s and 1930s, Ruth ran a primary school in the Unthank Road, combining discipline with humour and referring to herself as 'The Great Aunt', after the rather unpopular character in *Swallows and Amazons* by Arthur Ransome. At the start of the Second

World War, Ruth took on a more prominent role in public life, qualifying in 1941 as a Home Office ARP Instructor. Well known for her caring attitude and meticulous attention to detail, she was made honorary organiser of the Mutual Aid Good Neighbours' Association (MAGNA) in Norwich, formed to encourage co-operation with the ARP wardens and other voluntary organisations. On a surprise visit to Norwich on Tuesday, 13 October 1942, King George VI approached the uniformed Ruth. Having explained the acronym MAGNA on her shoulder badge, the King responded, 'Mrs Hardy, there is too little friendship in the world today; do keep up this wonderful work when the war is over.'[2]

In November 1945, Ruth was elected as a Labour Councillor for Heigham Ward in Norwich, and enlisted onto the prestigious Education, Health and Libraries committees, where she offered a lone, yet strident, female voice in a predominantly man's world. Bertie kept his head down at the school, sympathising with his browbeaten brother-in-law William, who was married to Ruth's formidable sister Emily.

Ruth excelled as a member of many governing bodies, including the East Anglian School for Deaf and Blind Children, Consolidated Charities and Norwich Festival Society. Five years on, the local press announced: 'The Norwich Labour Party is nominating Mrs Ruth Elsie Hardy as Lord Mayor of Norwich for 1950–51. If elected she will become only the third woman to hold the city's chief office and the first married woman to do so.'[3] Utilising her flirtatious smile and spontaneous wit, Ruth ensured she was voted in by her peers.

But Norwich City Council still had no official designation for a male consort. Bertie, uncomfortable with this new public prominence, agreed that unmarried daughter Marion would be the ideal substitute. Short-sighted, with pebble glasses similar to her father's, this clever, bossy, former head girl of Norwich High School, Oxford graduate and teacher of modern languages was willing to oblige. Taking leave of absence from the Perse School for Girls in Cambridge, Marion served as Lady Mayoress, an arrangement that suited Bertie very well. He did, however, have to suffer the taunts of his young pupils who, having up until then dubbed him 'Tosh', now insisted on referring to him as 'Lady Mayoress'.

Ruth already had a clear idea of her objectives. She immediately set about liberating the magnificent civic coach[4] from Strangers' Hall, where it had languished since 1939. Arthur and Colonel, dapple greys from the brewery stables of Steward & Patteson, were brought into service and a new suit of clothes was commissioned for the coachman, including a pair of silk stockings. Ruth was looking forward to the trappings of power and status, wearing the black and gold robes and the ancient chain of office, and convening with the famous, influential and wealthy. She came from among the lower ranks of society, but having risen to some eminence saw nothing wrong with enjoying the benefits.

On the morning of 23 May 1950, Ruth Hardy left her home at 9 Josephine Close in Town Close Ward, entering Norwich City Hall[5] as an elected councillor. She was to leave through the heavy bronze doors as the third female Lord Mayor of Norwich. In her acceptance speech she said:

> When first asked to accept this office I instantaneously ... refused. Until I realised that I was not doing something that I have repeatedly asked women to do, to help men shoulder the burden of local government. I believe there is a need for more and more women to give that inspiration and intuition which they possess, to help and solve the problems of local government.[6]

Shoppers and tourists cheered and clapped the 'Housewife Lord Mayor' as her diminutive figure, dressed in sweeping robes, descended City Hall steps and climbed aboard the coach. Accompanied by liveried attendants and escorted by police outriders, Ruth rode to the Maid's Head Hotel for the official inauguration banquet. Members of her family were there, including her great-nieces Christine, fourteen, and Tiggie, twelve, deemed mature enough to join such a momentous family occasion.

Ten days later, Ruth's official car, barely eight weeks old, was involved in an accident in Hillside Avenue in Thorpe St Andrew. Ruth was mercifully unhurt, but the civic car was badly damaged. On her arrival at a tea party, held in her honour by 100 members and twenty guests at the MAGNA Pensioner's Club in St Augustine's, her demeanour gave away nothing of the drama she had just faced. The club's Vice Chairman, Mr Chilvers, solved the problem of how to address a female Lord Mayor by referring to her as 'My Lady Lord Mayor'.[7] Ruth had no objection.

Plans were already well under way for the city's contributions to the much-anticipated Festival of Britain, Norwich chosen as one of only twenty-six cities in the UK to hold an official arts festival. As Lord Mayor, Ruth took over as Chairman of the Norwich Festival Society. Supervising progress for the Norwich programme of events taking place from 18 to 30 June 1951, she was proud to handwrite the invitation to Princess Elizabeth to open the festivities, painfully aware that by June 1951 she would no longer be Lord Mayor. Someone else would have the honour of greeting the King's eldest daughter to the city. Ruth was, however, invited to write a 'Lord Mayor's Message', to feature in the official guide to the festivities published by local printers Jarrold & Sons. The distinctive cover in grey, red and gold was designed by Tom Griffiths, married to Jessie Griffiths, who was destined to be next female Lord Mayor of the city in 1969. Ruth described Norwich as having 'the grace of a noble cathedral city, the bustle of a busy market town and the efficiency of a modern industrial centre'.[8]

Ruth was passionately loyal to the Royal Family, never failing to send greetings on the big occasions, including Queen Mary's eighty-third birthday and on the birth of Princess Anne in August 1950. She quickly proved adept at handling any situation, at ease, including ceremonial occasions and when meeting the elderly and the young. Her speech-making quickly became renowned for its depth of research and clarity of delivery. During December 1950 she worked every day, fulfilling festive engagements in hospitals, old people's homes and orphanages, her infectious laugh raising a smile wherever she went. On one occasion on visiting a school to watch a pantomime dress rehearsal, someone mistook Ruth's civic robes for a theatrical costume and ushered her into the dressing room. Despite her busy timetable, Ruth regularly found time for her beloved great-nieces and nephews. The youngsters gathered for exclusive tours of City Hall, the Guildhall and Norwich Castle, intrigued by the dungeons and battlements.

When Bertram Mills Circus arrived in Norwich on 9 April 1951, Christine and Tiggie were collected in the Lord Mayor's Humber Super Snipe and taken to Eaton Park to sit in the Lord Mayor's special box in the Big Top. Here they enjoyed a wire-walking lion, trapeze artistes, and the popular elephant ballet. Christine became quite anxious, fearing the huge animals might tip over backwards and squash her![9] Later that spring, Ruth, younger sister Beatrice and her two great-nieces attended a tea dance at the popular Samson & Hercules club in Tombland, Christine noting that her eccentric Great-Aunt Bea 'was the only one who danced'.

Ruth became adept at greeting royalty to the city. Towards the end of her mayoral year, on 24 April 1951, Queen Elizabeth arrived in the city to open a new wing at the Norwich Training College in Keswick Hall. The Queen had taken a great interest too in the refurbishment of the magnificent Georgian Assembly House in Theatre Street, reopened as a centre for arts during the previous November by the Lord Lieutenant[10] of Norfolk, Sir Edmund Bacon. This visit to Norwich offered an opportunity to see for herself the polished floors, graceful ceiling mouldings, the Music Room with its new platform and the antique cut-glass chandelier of thirty lights. Following lunch with the Bishop of Norwich, the Queen was driven to the Assembly House, Her Majesty unusually seated next to the chauffeur, watched by crowds of excited onlookers. First, the Bishop presented the Lord Mayor to Her Majesty, and in turn, Ruth presented Marion, who gave a well-rehearsed curtsey before handing the Queen a bouquet of pink roses and white heather.

Bertie was rightly proud of his wife's achievements. Although he was not her official consort, he felt honoured to accompany his wife to London for arguably the grandest weekend of events of her mayoral year. On the morning of Thursday, 3 May 1951, Bertie helped his wife into her gold and black robes and Lord Mayor's hat, before protocol demanded she walk unescorted up the steps of St Paul's Cathedral, to join a congregation of 3,000 for the interdenominational Service of Dedication for the long-awaited Festival of Britain. Following the solemnities, King George VI stood on the steps and officially declared the festivities open, saying that 'this Festival had been planned, like its predecessor in 1851, as a visible sign of national achievement and confidence.'[11]

Londoners woke the following morning to drizzle and low mist. Undeterred by the weather, thousands of invited guests, including Ruth and Bertie, turned out to explore the Festival site on the South Bank, marvelling at exhibits such as the Dome of Discovery and the Lion and Unicorn Pavilion. As Big Ben chimed 11.00 am, the King, Queen and Princess Margaret emerged from the official limousine, protected from the rain by footmen holding large umbrellas. They were greeted by a detachment of the 36th Army Engineer Regiment, duly inspected by His Majesty.

That evening, Ruth and Bertie, both suitably attired, entered the Mansion House, official residence of London's Lord Mayor. The Right Honourable Mr Alderman Denys Lowson welcomed Ruth as the only female Lord Mayor amongst the eighteen heads of civic authorities invited to this sumptuous Festival of Britain dinner. The instructions were clear: no chains of office to be worn, just badges. For Ruth this was no hardship. She explained to reporters: 'As I do not have a waistcoat button to which the chain can be secured, a special guard chain has to be hung around my neck, which during a lengthy function, can be extremely painful.'[12]

Following the meal, taken in the company of the Labour Prime Minister, Clement Attlee, guests endured a depressing speech about the dangers of the Cold War, from Foreign Secretary Herbert Morrison, before the contingent of mayors, some of whom were women, were presented with boxes of cigarettes. The rather more elevated Lord Mayors received cigars. When asked if she would like to exchange the gift, Ruth refused, returning home with the decorative box, despite her being a lifelong campaigner against smoking.

Just three weeks later, on 23 May 1951, Ruth passed her robes, hat and chain to the incoming Lord Mayor, Mr Eric Hindle. The following week, a female reporter from the local press arrived at Ruth's home to find her dressed in a 'tailored pearl grey house frock, answering correspondence'. In reply to a question about the public's perception of her role, she said:

> I think people visualise a Lord Mayor's life as a succession of banquets and parties. Actually I very often missed lunch altogether through talking past one o'clock to the many overseas visitors who come to look at the Lord Mayor's Parlour and civic regalia. I did manage to keep reasonable hours, however, by saying quite frankly that I would like to leave dinners and evening functions at ten o'clock.

The interviewer persisted: 'But how did you manage to keep up such a spruce appearance?'

Ruth's reply was:

> I simply invested in a really good black barathea mohair suit, which doesn't crumple or look jaded after a day's wear, and rang the changes with hats and blouses. My maxim is 'Never sit about in good clothes; change as soon as you get home.'[13]

Ruth remained a city councillor, retaining a strong interest in politics, stalwartly supporting many Norwich groups, particularly in health and education. She was much impressed by the rising star of the Conservative Party, Margaret Thatcher, predicting, 'Mark my words, she will be a great prime minister.'[14]

Bertie died in the Norfolk and Norwich Hospital on 15 May 1966, aged seventy-eight. In 1970, Ruth stepped down from her council seat, retiring to Foulgers House in Bracondale, an assisted home for the elderly, taking the adjacent flat to her sister Beatrice. Ruth died on 7 February 1975, aged eighty-five. Her spirited approach to life was much missed by the family.

Her daughter Marion remained a lifelong spinster, retiring as Principal of Hatfield Polytechnic. Returning to Norwich, she lived in Christchurch Road, and resolved to re-establish links with close family members. But it was too little too late; nephews and nieces had grown up and moved on.[15] She died alone from cancer aged sixty-six in May 1988, bequeathing nearly £160,000 to Oxfam. Amongst Marion's effects were two bound leather volumes, inherited from her mother, filled with newspaper cuttings, menus, brochures, invitations, telegrams and photographs, cataloguing every detail of the year that Ruth and Marion had shared together in civic office. Inside a crumpled envelope addressed to Ruth at her modest city home was a handwritten note dated 19 May 1951. It was signed by Sir Edmund Bacon, scribed on the embossed letterhead of Raveningham Hall, the ancestral home of the Bacon family since 1735, illustrating how well Ruth Elsie Peachey, the daughter of a country gamekeeper, had successfully bridged the rigid class divide of the early 1950s:

> My dear Lord Mayor,
>
> I feel I must send you a line to say how very sad I feel that your term of office as Lord Mayor of Norwich is shortly coming to an end. In the long line of mayors and Lord Mayors of Norwich a few may possibly have equalled but none could have excelled the way in which you have carried through your Lord Mayoralty. Would you, along with Mr Hardy and your daughter, care to come to lunch here on Sunday, 3 June at 1.00 pm? I do hope you will be able to manage it and for once be able to have a meal without having to make a speech at the end of it.
>
> Yours very sincerely,
>
> Edmund Bacon.

Endnotes

1. Anderson, Andrew, memories of his aunts, email 21 July 2015.
2. Banger, Joan, *Norwich At War*, Albion Books, Norwich, 1974. Reprinted 1982.
3. *Eastern Daily Press*, 3 May 1950. Ruth was also the first socialist female Lord Mayor.
4. The black horse-drawn coach was given to the city by Sir Eustace Gurney in 1911 and once used for a visit to Norwich by King George V. Built between 1830 and 1838, it became a regular sight at civic events, each year

used to transport key figures to the Justice service in honour of a visiting High Court judge. Out of action for two years due to moth infestation, it was revived in October 2011, during the mayoral year of Jenny Lay. Its last outing was in 2015 for Brenda Arthur. Sadly, with no budget for the necessary refurbishment, the coach is currently stored in Strangers' Hall.

5. Ruth was the first lady Lord Mayor of Norwich to work in the new City Hall. During the early twentieth century, Norwich Guildhall was deemed too small to cope. As early as 1908, a proposal to demolish the ancient Guildhall was only defeated by the Mayor's casting vote. In 1928, the Council began buying up land and disused shops and dwellings close to the Market Square. A distinguished architect, Mr Robert Atkinson, was appointed to supervise the building of a new municipal office building and in 1931 a design competition was launched attracting 143 entries. The winners were C.H. James and S. Rowland Pierce from a London firm of architects. On Saturday, 29 October 1938, the largest crowd ever seen in Norwich assembled in the Market Square to witness Lord Mayor Charles Watling invite King George VI and Queen Elizabeth to open this magnificent Art Deco building, the King remarking that it was the foremost public building to be built between the wars. It is believed that Adolf Hitler would have chosen the building to be his regional headquarters had he won the Second World War.

6. *Eastern Evening News*, 23 May 1950.

7. Following the Second World War, Ruth's welfare work continued with her forming the hugely successful MAGNA Old-Age Pensioners Club in St Augustine's, eventually becoming its life president.

8. *The Book of the Norwich Festival*, published by Norwich Festival Society Ltd, 1951.

9. Sutherland, Christine, email 14 July 2015.

10. Lord Lieutenants are appointed for each county as the Queen's representative, overseeing arrangements for all Royal visits, presenting medals and awards, advising on submissions for honours nominations and preparing the guest lists for Royal Garden Parties. He or she also appoints Deputy Lieutenants in Norfolk, who represent the Lord Lieutenant at important events when required. One of these is given the role of Vice Lord Lieutenant. The non-political and unpaid positions continue until an incumbent reaches the age of seventy-five.

11. *Eastern Daily Press*, 4 May 1951.

12. *Ibid.*

13. *Eastern Daily Press*, 'Over the Tea-Table' column, 24 May 1951.

14. https://joemasonspage.wordpress.com. Published 26 February 2017. Joe Mason is Ruth's great-nephew.

15. 'After centuries of catching rabbits around West Suffolk, something

remarkable happened to the family in the twentieth century. Of Phipp Peachey's children, grandchildren and great-grandchildren, there have been a Lord Mayor, an architect, the deputy head of a public school and a university professor. Others have been health professionals and teachers. At least seven of his descendants have gone to Oxbridge universities. In one or two generations, the family had moved from the poorest of the working class to the upper ranks of the middle class.' https://joemasonspage. wordpress.com, published 16 December 2013.

Ruth Elsie Hardy 1950–51

Further Highlights from her Mayoral Year

- Meeting with old friends and colleagues at the tea party given by MAGNA Pensioners' Club in her honour, at the group's headquarters in St Augustine's.

- Presenting a bouquet to Mr & Mrs Arthur Blanchard, both seventy-eight, on the occasion of their diamond wedding anniversary. Joking with Mr Blanchard, 'You don't often get a kiss from a Lord Mayor.'

- Representing Norwich in a civic procession held in Ipswich to commemorate the granting of its first borough charter by King John 750 years previously. Meeting civic dignitaries from nine other East Anglian boroughs.

- Enjoying a lunch of Scotch salmon with lobster mayonnaise, with King George VI, Queen Elizabeth and Princess Margaret in the Royal Pavilion at the Royal Norfolk Show, held for the first time at Amner, part of the King's Sandringham Estate. Being amused when the Queen presented her husband with the King's Lynn Challenge Cup for the best group of Red Poll cattle.

- Mingling with 6,000 guests at a Royal Garden Party at Buckingham Palace, including Harold Wilson and Minister of Health Aneurin Bevan.

- Taking the salute at Norwich Cathedral of over 600 RAF men from Norwich airfields, attending the tenth anniversary Battle of Britain thanksgiving service.

- Opening the Home Lovers' Exhibition in Blackfriars Hall, noting in her speech that 'We housewives notice with much satisfaction that goods we missed so very much during the war are coming back into our shops.'

- Launching a public appeal for over £20,000 to maintain the fabric of Norwich Cathedral over the following fifteen years, commenting that, 'The cathedral is ours. It belongs to every man, woman and child in Norwich and I appeal to them to help in its preservation.'

- Presenting the winners' trophy of the second division of the National Speedway League, to Paddy (Crash) Mills, captain of Norwich Stars Speedway Club at the Lido Ballroom.

- Posing as a photographers' model during a portraiture session at the Norwich and District Photographic Society, having agreed to do so when opening the society's exhibition, and offering a prize for the best print of the evening.

CHAPTER 4

Jessie Ruby Griffiths (1904–1992)

Lord Mayor of Norwich 1969–70

A man whose body was pulled out of the river Yare on Sunday has been identified as a well-known local artist, whose work was displayed in many Norwich and London exhibitions. Tom Griffiths, 88-year-old husband of former city Lord Mayor Jessie Griffiths, went missing from his Essex Street home during stormy weather on 23 January. Sgt Keith Teesdale of Norwich Police said that two people had spotted Mr Griffiths walking in Trowse, after an appeal for the missing man was put out through the media. He immediately recognised Mr Griffiths, who had three fingers missing from his right hand, when his body was pulled out of the river.

(*Eastern Daily Press*, 14 February 1990)

Conservative Councillor Jessie Ruby Griffiths was a woman of uncompromising views with a sharp edge to her tongue. She was not easily browbeaten and perfectly capable of challenging her political opponents during meetings of Norwich City Council. Her frequent stormy exchanges with Labour Leader Arthur South raised eyebrows throughout the Chamber. Many thought that Arthur had a sneaky regard for his adversary, and was openly amused when she once publicly denounced him as a 'Champagne socialist'.[1]

In November 1923, as Ethel Colman became the first lady Lord Mayor of Norwich, 19-year-old Jessie West joined the staff of Norwich

Corporation. She enquired about joining the National Association of Local Government Officers (NALGO), but was dismayed to find that women were barred from becoming members. She rallied the female workforce, her quick brain devising a strategy before putting their case to union officials. By 1925, she and six other women had been added to the membership.

The second daughter of Norwich carpenter Edmund West, Jessie was a woman of many parts: talented seamstress, accomplished cook, lover of classical music and a freelance writer, publishing articles and short stories under the pen name Jane Archer. But on her wedding day on 12 September 1931, much of that was in the future. Her groom was Tom Griffiths, a Norwich boy who was working as an illustrator in London. The couple joined hands at the chapel in the Field Congregational Church,[2] overlooking Chapelfield Gardens, while Tom's uncle, accomplished musician and choirmaster George Percival Griffiths, played the organ music for the ceremony. Tom was born in 1901, mercifully too young to fight in the Great War. However, poignantly missing from the 'groom's side' was his mother, Eva, who died in 1923, and his older brother, Lewis Herbert, Second Lieutenant Norfolk Regiment, killed in action on 11 September 1918, only weeks before the end of the conflict, aged just eighteen. It was left to Uncle George and Tom's father, Herbert, a builder with Norwich Corporation, to represent the Griffiths family.

Tom was intelligent, modest, likeable and a gentle man. In his teenage years he had helped to pull a boat up a slipway near Southwold and, pulling on the wrong wire, had lost three fingers on his right hand. His ambition had been to join the Royal Navy, but this injury put a stop to that. Despite discouragement from his father, he studied at Norwich School of Art and the Heatherley School of Fine Art in London, holding his brush between his one finger and thumb. It was here that he discovered his extraordinary talent for creating intricate vellum illuminations, a skill that would keep him employed for the whole of his life.[3] For the first ten years of marriage, Tom and Jessie lived in London, returning to Norwich in 1939, when Tom joined the staff at Norwich School of Art[4] and Jessie took a post working with the Food Ministry. Here she learnt how to deal with different types of people.

> As Assistant Food Officer for Norwich my duties covered supervision of the public office. When counter staff became exasperated by difficult customers … they were passed on to me.

> We met everyone from gypsies and tramps to countesses; even famous film stars had to collect their special touring ration cards from us.[5]

Alongside his teaching job, Tom set up a small studio in their modest Essex Street home. By the summer of 1954 he had enough canvasses to exhibit at the Norwich Artists' Exhibition at the Assembly House, his paintings attracting much interest. Two months previously, Tom was elected a Fellow of the Royal Society of Arts, his elevated status delighting his upwardly mobile wife. Perhaps seeking to match his achievement, Jessie stood as a Conservative candidate for the City Council seat of Town Close in 1955. Her twenty years' work as a public servant meant she had no fear of the Council Chamber, explaining that as a private citizen she had been appalled by the Labour Party's use of the 'block vote'. Her understanding was that on the Conservative benches a councillor was free to vote according to his or her conscience and knowledge.

Jessie served for two years before losing her seat in 1957, then standing again in 1959, this time for Nelson Ward. In her adoption speech she explained why, if elected, she would be voting against a new central library or covered swimming pool: 'I could not, with a clear conscience, vote for these two items while the slum clearance problem is still unresolved.' The housing problems of the city that had occupied both Ethel Colman and Mabel Clarkson were still high on the local agenda. Jessie was a hands-on councillor, paying visits to the struggling housewives and mothers on the Tuckswood estate and other council properties, always heartened to be welcomed as an empathetic woman.

During the late 1950s, Tom was fully committed to many months of work as he completed his most prestigious commission to date: to inscribe the names of more than 5,000 Norfolk men and women who died during the Second World War into a leather-bound vellum roll of honour and illuminating the opening pages in full colour, featuring the arms of county, city and boroughs. The book was destined to be on permanent display in Norwich Cathedral. The Bishop of Norwich led the service of dedication on 16 July 1958, an event attended by Queen Elizabeth the Queen Mother and 1,700 guests. Although Jessie was not a councillor at that time, as the wife of the artist she was able to bask in Tom's reflected glory.

The marriage produced no children, and with Tom spending his time expanding his portfolio, Jessie immersed herself in council work, serving on committees related to museums, parks, staff and wages, and children. She was the first woman to serve on the Eastern Electricity Consultative Council and on the Norwich Health Executive Council. Despite his increasing fame, Tom's financial rewards were limited and the couple continued to live modestly in their Victorian semi-detached house on Essex Street. When out in company Jessie was insecure about her distinctive Norwich accent, regretting her lack of formal education. She watched with envy as the Norwich Conservative elite enjoyed their relative wealth, living a lifestyle to which she could only aspire.

In 1963, Jessie was made Deputy to Lord Mayor Leonard Howes, followed a year later with her nomination as the first female Conservative Sheriff of Norwich. This honour resulted in a new artistic venture for Tom, which endured for nearly twenty-five years. The City Council presented civics with a leather-bound visitors' book with the city crest embossed in gold on the front. Outgoing Lord Mayors and Sheriffs were welcome to keep them as mementos. Beginning with Jessie's book as Sheriff, year after year Tom would illustrate the opening pages with an image of the city crest, flanked by angels, and the recipient's name and dates beautifully inscribed on the opposite leaf. During her civic year, Jessie indulged her penchant for hats, and was forced to take seasickness pills before riding in the civic coach. She took advantage of her official engagements to highlight her real concerns about the 'pockets of squalor' around the city and the disappearance of little shops and characterful pubs. She explained to the Norwich Rotary Club with her customary ferocity: 'If I had the power, I would go out, buy an enormous broom and sweep the city clean.'

Eleven years after becoming a councillor, Jessie was elected as an alderman, with only one person having voted against the appointment. In the Chamber that day was former Lord Mayor Ruth Hardy, welcomed back to City Hall after a period of illness. As an alderman, Jessie was now considered a high-ranking member of the Council, entitled to serve but no longer representing a ward. At a party held by the Nelson Ward branch committee of Norwich Conservative Association, Jessie was presented with a crystal vase and a bouquet, tokens of appreciation for her services to the ward since 1959. Kevin Fitzmaurice,[6] a Rotarian and successful local businessman, was elected to her seat.

With these honours bestowed upon her, Jessie's ambition to become First Citizen seemed a little closer. It was three years before her subtle but persistent lobbying resulted in her nomination as the fourth lady Lord Mayor of Norwich. At her inauguration in City Hall, the public gallery was untypically less than half full. In her acceptance speech, Jessie spoke of her desire to see a purpose-built conference centre built in the city and of her aim to be the 'City Council's public relations officer' to explain the workings of local government at every appropriate opportunity. Before taking her place for photographs on the City Hall steps, Jessie broke with tradition, nominating Tom as her official consort. In doing so, she became the first female Lord Mayor not to be accompanied by a Lady Mayoress.[7]

No one was more surprised than Councillor Fitzmaurice when the Lord Mayor Elect approached him some weeks before Mayor-Making. Jessie suggested he might like to be her deputy. Kevin discussed it with his wife Theresa before accepting the offer, having been rather taken aback when Jessie had declared she had chosen him because of his big car and because he had enough money in his pocket not to have to claim expenses. To this day, Kevin is not sure if she was joking. Jessie's capacity for tact was invariably lacking. She upset Theresa when instructing her never to be seen without hat and gloves when out in the city. It was Jessie's peremptory tone that made it sound not so much a request as an order. Her controlling tendencies were also apparent when chairing council meetings, warning colleagues, somewhat tongue in cheek: 'I don't intend to allow anyone to behave as I have done on occasions.'

Jessie was resilient, determined to do the job just as men had done. She particularly enjoyed invitations to functions where she was the sole woman, her presence only permitted because of her official role – the largest such function having 550 men in attendance. She admitted that she found the chain and robes to be a constant hindrance, but she had developed a philosophy: 'Whenever the chains and robes seem most uncomfortable, I remind myself how many other people would like to be wearing them.' Despite her abrasive demeanour, Jessie loved to entertain, always using the Lord Mayor's Parlour and taking a personal interest in the menus, table settings and flower arrangements. Her home was too small and over-filled with artists' materials and canvasses to even consider hosting functions there.

During Jessie's year in office, Tom and Kevin became close friends, Kevin calling in at Tom's tiny studio to watch him painting, while the two men 'put the world to rights'. Tom was adept at capturing local scenes, both urban and rural, and Kevin would often buy his latest work before the paint was even dry. Jessie was fully occupied enjoying the trappings of pomp while associating with professors, MPs and bishops. With Tom rarely far away, Jessie hosted a buffet lunch at City Hall for academic staff from the University of East Anglia during its graduation week; was guest speaker at the Norfolk Federation of Women's Institutes Annual Meeting; wore a sprig of shamrock at a St Patrick Night's dinner; and welcomed Princess Alexandra to City Hall, overlooked by hundreds of staff and councillors who packed the balcony above.

With her heavy dark eyebrows, tight perm, generous chins and stocky build, Jessie appeared formidable, but once she turned on her smile, her well-practised charm offensive offered reassurance to her hosts. She was even seen to be coquettish when greeting distinguished gentlemen. Alongside the elderly and the very young, Jessie seemed more relaxed, with her smile genuine and her eyes kind. Kevin found himself deputising at events that were either double booked, or those that both Jessie or her Sheriff, George Moyes, preferred not to attend – invariably annual general meetings, sports days and boring dinners.

By May 1970, Tom was anxious to return full time to his easel. He had stalwartly supported his wife, smiling for the cameras, holding the handbag, but the commissions were mounting up. Jessie was also missing her work, admitting that, as Lord Mayor, she had found it difficult to remain impartial when chairing meetings and was looking forward to returning to 'the arena'. In June 1971, following an internal dispute within her party, Jessie was made Leader of the Conservative Opposition, becoming the first woman leader of a political party in the history of Norwich City Council. She held the position until 1976, standing down from the Council in 1978, aged seventy-five. Still active, Jessie retained many of her committee responsibilities in the city, notably as President of the Norwich Organisation of Active Help (NOAH), a group of volunteers, the majority being young people, working under the auspices of the management committee with support from Norfolk Youth and Community Service and Norfolk Social Services. In December 1977, Jessie had been delighted to accept a cheque for £5,000 on behalf of NOAH, presented by Lord Mayor Ralph Roe, as they posed for photographs under the huge council Christmas tree outside City Hall.[8]

In Essex Street the doorbell sounded. Jessie wasn't answering. Tom would have to leave his easel to see who it was. On the doorstep were the Mayor and Mayoress of King's Lynn, William and Kathleen Baker. It was October 1980, and Jessie had been keeping this visit a secret from her husband for almost a month. The esteemed guests bore gifts: a memento bearing the Lynn coat of arms for Tom, a copy of the Magna Carta for Jessie. The Mayor wanted to thank Tom in person for his work over twenty-eight years, designing and preparing intricate illuminated civic records for the town. In 1954, King's Lynn had bestowed the Freedom of the City upon Queen Elizabeth the Queen Mother, presenting her with 'a truly beautiful vellum'. For more than two decades, each outgoing mayor received an 'In Appreciation' scroll, commemorating his or her year in office. Tom modestly accepted the praise from his esteemed visitors.

Norwich and King's Lynn were not the only places to benefit from Tom's skills and talent. Over the following ten years his order book was continually full, with him producing illuminated scrolls and visitors' books for councils in Thetford, Great Yarmouth and Beccles, as well as for regiments of the British Army and the University of East Anglia. He relaxed by painting scenes of Norwich, his favourite subjects being the Guildhall, the church of St Peter Mancroft, Norwich Market and most of the other churches, many being depicted in night scenes.[9]

Jessie's final 'hurrah' came in 1981, when she was made an MBE for services to local government in Norwich. It must have felt like the pinnacle of a life devoted to public service. She could now concentrate on enjoying the fruits of her husband's lauded career. However, as time went on, Jessie became isolated, rarely leaving her home. She had no family and few friends, her quarrelsome attitude tending to drive people away. As the years passed, her health deteriorating, she spent her days in a wheelchair in the front room, bitter over her decline and envious of Tom's continuing success. She was a proud woman, instructing Tom not to tell a soul about her condition. She became totally dependent upon her husband for her every need, and was increasingly belligerent and demanding.

By 1990, Tom was unable to cope. At eighty-eight he was suffering with debilitating back pain and a suspected hernia, and was depressed by increasing thoughts of being trapped. One bitterly cold and stormy January day, he took a walk to the river Yare at Postwick and waded into the water. The coroner recorded an open verdict. He could not be satisfied beyond reasonable doubt that Mr Griffiths had deliberately killed himself. The newspaper reported that Tom was under the impression he had an incurable disease and had chosen to end his life. But friends closest to him knew differently. With Tom's demise, Jessie could no longer remain in her home. Her former deputy, Kevin, stepped in, arranging to sell the property, clear her belongings and secure Jessie a place in a Brundall nursing home. She lived there quietly for nearly two years, until her death in March 1992, aged eighty-seven.

In happier times, Jessie never failed to acknowledge her husband's talent and good nature. During her many interviews with the press following her Mayor-Making in 1969, Jessie made this prophetic statement:

> Long after I am remembered only by a name carved in stone outside the Council Chamber, some of Tom's work will remain; things like the War Memorial Book of Remembrance in the cathedral, and the work he did on the Eagle Roof of the Great Hospital, painted with such perfection that old and new could not be distinguished.

Endnotes

1. Kevin Fitzmaurice, speaking in 2016.
2. The church, with its twin towers and circular rose window, fell into disrepair and was demolished in 1972.
3. His cover design for the 1951 Norwich Festival, the city's contribution to the Festival of Britain, first brought Tom's work into the public domain.
4. Tom finished his teaching career as a senior lecturer in Graphic Design, leaving Norwich School of Art in 1950 to become a freelance artist.
5. *Eastern Daily Press*, 29 May 1963.
6. Kevin Fitzmaurice resigned from the City Council in 1970, following an invitation to become a magistrate (possibly the first Catholic magistrate in Norwich since the Reformation). Fitzmaurice Carriers Limited is a long-established and well-known family business in the city.
7. Ethel Colman and Mabel Clarkson both asked their sisters to be consort. Ruth Hardy gave the honour to her daughter.
8. The organisation would later evolve into Voluntary Norfolk.
9. His paintings continue to become available for sale in galleries all over the country.

Jessie Ruby Griffiths 1969–70

Further Highlights from her Mayoral Year

- Opening the new Terminal at Norwich Airport with a visit inside an aircraft alongside members of the Air Cadets.

- Hosting a retirement reception for the Dean of Norwich, the Very Reverend Norman Hook, an eminent author.

- Meeting both the Chief Rabbi Dr Immanuel Jacobovitz and actor and storyteller David Kossoff, at the consecration of the new Jewish Synagogue in Earlham Road.

- Presenting the trophies at the RAF Bowls Final in RAF Coltishall and linking arms for the camera with two young officers.

- Enjoying canapés and wine at the tenth anniversary celebration of the Norfolk and Norwich Rouen Friendship Association.

- Opening the new Games Room at Norwich Lads' Club and being shown around the facilities for boxing, wrestling and football.

- Presenting Duke of Edinburgh Awards on a cold December day in her fabulous fur-trimmed overcoat.

- Attending a performance of *Goldilocks and the Three Bears*, the pantomime at Theatre Royal, starring singer Ronnie Hilton and wrestler Jackie Pallo, in the company of a group of Norwich pensioners.

- Taking a trip down the river Yare from Hardley Cross, aboard the historic wherry *Albion*. Meeting with members of Norfolk Wherry Trust.

- Greeting Her Royal Highness Princess Alexandra to City Hall, watched by councillors and staff crowded along the length of the balcony.

- Hosting a grand buffet in City Hall, with candelabra and best china, for academics from the University of East Anglia, to celebrate graduation week.

- Presenting John Jarrold, as incoming Lord Mayor, with a book signed by the directors and employees of Jarrold & Son Limited, marking the 200-year anniversary of the Jarrold story. Hearing how in 1770 the first John Jarrold opened a grocer's and draper's in the Market Place at Woodbridge in Suffolk.

CHAPTER 5

Joyce Lilian Morgan
(1922–2012)

Lord Mayor of Norwich 1975–76

I used to get to ride in the official car. One day, Nan arranged for my friend Julie and me to go to school in it, with all the flags flying. Nan wasn't with us. It was so exciting. I was always in the Lord Mayor's Parlour. I practically had the run of the building, in and out of the Council Chamber. It was like having my own personal playground.

(Selina Tobin, née Morgan, speaking in 2016)

From day one of her civic year in May 1975, Labour Councillor Joyce Morgan actively involved her 9-year-old granddaughter Selina in the pomp and ceremony of her role. Selina adored wearing her grandmother's gowns, her jewellery and even the Lord Mayor's badge. Occasionally for an evening event, Nan would allow her to wear a pair of normally forbidden high heels. One afternoon, Selina and her friends from the Eighth Norwich Brownie Pack took tea in the Mayor's Parlour, each little girl signing her name in the visitor's book. It could also be embarrassing having your grandmother as the centre of public attention. When Joyce presided over the 'Topping Out' ceremony for the new Four Schools' Swimming Pool in Recreation Road, Selina was amongst the pupils from Heigham Park First School. They looked on astonished as the Lord Mayor, wearing white shoes and sunglasses,

36

climbed onto the flat roof of the partially completed building, to join a gang of builders celebrating with the traditional glass of beer!

On the completion in 1966 of Normandie Tower, a high rise block of flats at the foot of Rouen Road in Norwich, Joyce and Welsh-born husband Gwilym moved into Flat 86 on the fourteenth floor, and were captivated by the view of the city beyond. It was here that Selina was born on 28 July 1967. Her mother Sandra, having opted for a home delivery, chose her mother-in-law's home for the birth, with Joyce on hand offering hot flannels and encouragement. Joyce remained very much a 'hands-on' grandmother, regularly helping Sandra with babysitting, outings and school runs. When Joyce was honoured by the City Council, there was no way 8-year-old Selina would miss out on the fun.

Within a few months of moving in, Joyce was instrumental in setting up the Normandie Tower Community Association, serving as Chairman for many years. A vacant ground floor flat was converted into a communal area to hold concerts, whist drives, table tennis games and coffee mornings. Later, a small hair salon and lending library were added. Joyce made it her business to support, advise and befriend residents, many of them elderly, whatever time of day or night. She became quite the matriarch. During her year as Lord Mayor, Normandie Tower residents enjoyed many social outings with their esteemed neighbour, including drinking tea from gold-crested china cups in the Lord Mayor's Parlour and taking a tour of Watney's Brewery. A visit to a recording of the popular quiz show *Sale of the Century* at Anglia TV studios culminated in a group photograph, featuring ebullient compère Nicolas Parsons seated between Joyce and Gwilym.

During those twelve months, Selina shared the limelight with her grandfather Gwilym, Joyce's husband of thirty-two years. Gwilym revelled in his role as consort to a high-profile political woman, the family joking that he modelled himself on Denis Thatcher. Always the dandy and enjoying a gin and tonic or three, Gwilym found official hospitality much to his liking. During an official two-day excursion touring East Anglia, Margaret Thatcher MP, the new Leader of the Conservative Party,[1] arrived in Norwich on 14 November. That morning, these two formidable women, from opposing political parties – both with remarkably similar blonde permanent waves – met in the Lord Mayor's Parlour. Gwilym took this opportunity to shake Denis's hand. Before leaving City Hall, both visitors signed their names in the red leather-bound visitors' book. Formalities over, Mrs Thatcher embarked on a brisk ten-minute walkabout in Norwich Market, directly beneath City Hall, observed closely by staff and councillors from every accessible window.[2]

Much of Joyce's early childhood was spent in the impoverished old courts and yards of the city, notorious for overcrowded conditions, poor ventilation, lack of sanitation and natural sunlight. Born on 10 January 1922, in White Entry Yard, just off Magdalen Street, Joyce's father was Frederick Arthur Bird. He was a veteran of the Great War, during which he trained mules to carry military equipment in France. On his return home he became a self-taught electrician, while making and repairing boots and shoes for his family and neighbours. He met his wife, Mary Ann Barnes (known as Polly), when she was fourteen. During their marriage she gave birth to four children. Joyce was their third child, behind Ethel and Arthur and ahead of Stella. In 1926, their home, like thousands of others, was subject to the widespread slum clearance of the day. The Bird family was relocated to The Avenues, a pleasant residential street, and they were thrilled to discover that their new house had the rare luxury of an indoor bathroom and toilet. Baby Geoffrey (known as Dickie), was born in 1929, and in 1933 a sixth and final child arrived, William James, named after his father but known for the rest of his life as Terry – a nickname given by his older sisters Joyce and Ethel, both refusing to call the boy William.

Neighbours soon began referring to Mary Ann as the 'Lady of the Avenues', intrigued by her high standards of personal appearance and dress, never being seen without a hat. She told her sons, 'Providing your hair is well cut and combed and your shoes are cleaned, you don't have to worry about your suit, providing you have a nice tie on.'[3] Joyce was sent out shopping before school with one shilling in her pocket. With this she bought six pennyworth of meat such as brisket or sausages, as well as potatoes and a cabbage, an ample midday meal for the whole family. The tuppence change fed the gas meter. Joyce left school at fourteen to take up various jobs, including in the city boot and shoe trade, as an usherette at the Haymarket Cinema, and in 1939 at Caley's chocolate factory, where within six weeks, management promoted her to supervisor.

But with the outbreak of the Second World War, Joyce had to rethink her future, volunteering in 1940, aged eighteen, for the Women's Auxillary Air Force (WAAF). She was posted to Bomber Command Station at RAF Marham, near King's Lynn in Norfolk. Assigned to the sergeant's mess, waitressing and preparing rations for aircrew missions, one night she packed extra cheese sandwiches for her 'favourite boys', only to learn some hours later that the crew had ditched in the North Sea. Fearing the worst, Joyce was delighted to receive a telegram saying, 'All safe but sandwiches laid heavy!' Joyce kept that telegram for decades amongst her keepsakes. A while later, Joyce was promoted from aircraftswoman to corporal, and her responsibilities included taking parades, drilling and discipline. She especially enjoyed organising the WAAF entertainments, including popular station dances.

On the evening of 27 April 1942, during the first night of the Norwich Blitz, the Bird home in The Avenues was hit by German incendiary bombs.[4] Joyce and Stella were away, but brother Arthur, a serving soldier, was home on leave. At the all-clear the family emerged from the Anderson shelter to find the front of their home blown away, windows gone and curtains in shreds. Every house had suffered the same fate. The casualties were heavy: 162 killed that night in Norwich.[5] Arthur Bird helped for three days searching for people buried beneath the rubble, eventually rescuing young Jackie, a friend of the family, who later lost her leg. The City Council rewarded Arthur with a citation for his part in the rescue effort.

In the spring of 1943, Joyce married Gwilym Morgan, a colleague from RAF Marham. Her new status meant her immediate demobilisation. Their only son John was born on 13 February 1944. Joyce would have loved a daughter, and was unprepared for a boy. When her son arrived she said, 'Let's just call him John.' Gwilym immediately relocated his family to the relative safety of his home territory, the Rhondda Valley in South Wales. For three years, Joyce witnessed a level of deprivation, poverty and misery amongst the coalmining families, worse even than that experienced in the Norwich Yards. On their return to Norfolk, shortly after the end of the war, Gwilym joined the Norwich aircraft manufacturer Boulton & Paul as a storeman, whilst Joyce became a member of the Labour Party, concerned to abolish the 11-plus exam and to improve the lives of working people. She trained with St John Ambulance, developing an interest in the sick and in health issues, leading later to eighteen years' association with Norwich Health Authority.

Joyce represented the Labour Party at meetings of the Norwich Trades Council, sitting in debates alongside officials from local trade unions, one of very few women involved in union work at that level. Here she first met Joe Stirling, the Secretary Agent for the Labour Party in Norwich. She admired the young man's spirit and his common sense. At that time she had no idea of his former life as a Jewish boy in Nazi Germany, nor that, over a decade later, their paths would cross again.[6] Joyce became a city councillor for the first time in 1962, winning a seat on Bowthorpe Ward with a majority of 500 votes. Over the next four years she was called to sit on many local government selection panels, often finding herself as the only woman. When working-class bricklayer Henry Waters applied for an office job at City Hall, Joyce recommended him and, against the advice of some male colleagues, Henry was offered the role. He proved to be conscientious, and was later promoted to Public Health Inspector. His son Alan was destined to become a Labour councillor and Leader of Norwich City Council.

Joyce's political career flourished; she chaired committees with responsibility for children, welfare, education, housing and environmental health. In 1967, Joyce was proud to be appointed a magistrate, serving for nearly twenty-five years. During 1969, Joyce's father Frederick became ill with inoperable cancer. The prognosis was poor, so much so that the Army paid for youngest son Terry to travel home from his posting in Germany to say his goodbyes. Frederick passed away in January 1970, aged seventy-five. Nearly two years later, at the end of 1971, his widow Mary Ann died alone while watching Tommy Cooper on the television. Arthur Bird was passing her house on his way home after an evening out and saw his mother's house lights were out. Thinking she must have gone to bed, he decided not to call in. In fact, the electricity meter had run out of money. Mary Ann's body was not discovered until the following morning. Happily she had lived long enough to witness earlier in the year her daughter Joyce appointed as Deputy Lord Mayor of Norwich.

Early in 1974, the year appropriately designated as International Women's Year, the *Eastern Evening News* announced that Joyce Morgan was to be the fifth woman to hold Norwich's top civic job. Past Lord Mayor Donald Pratt spoke in support of her nomination, applauding her record of serving the old, the young and the sick. Councillor Jessie Griffiths, Lord Mayor in 1969, added: 'The job of Lord Mayor is a formidable undertaking for a woman. Everything is just a little bit harder than it is for a man, but women have tremendous stamina and resilience.'[7]

As she stood posing for photographs alongside the new Sheriff of Norwich, her old Labour Party friend Joe Stirling,[8] Joyce may well have reflected on those words. Her task ahead would certainly be challenging, not least in deciding exactly which outfit to wear, with so many events in the civic diary. But Joyce did have an advantage. She had a part-time job as a staff supervisor in the Norwich branch of fashion retailer C&A on the Haymarket. The local store management graciously put dozens of frocks and accessories at her disposal, new designs arriving at each change of season. There was one awkward 'garment' moment only two days following Mayor-Making. At the traditional 'At Home' evening reception, hosted by the new civics, the queue of guests shuffling towards Joyce in order to shake her hand seemed to stretch on forever. Observant onlookers suddenly noticed that one lady was wearing an identical gown to that of the new Lord Mayor. What would happen once the two ladies came face to face? Joyce and her guest dealt with the situation admirably, each politely ignoring the innocent faux pas.

Margaret Thatcher was not the only well-known dignitary to visit Norwich during Joyce's year of office. Joyce was particularly proud of the page of her visitor's book dated Tuesday, 1 July, bearing just one signature: 'Philip'. The Duke of Edinburgh was visiting the acclaimed Heritage over the Wensum project. Joyce, her hair styled by friend and hairdresser Jill Miller,[9] and wearing white gloves with matching handbag, accompanied the Royal visitor on an Edwardian steam launch – aptly named the *Princess Margaret* – during its short journey from Foundry Bridge to Friar's Quay, with cheering onlookers lining the banks of the Wensum. Following an extensive walkabout in the sunshine, shaking hands with every representative from the Housing Development Project, the Duke and Joyce called into the Woolpack Public House for some 'refreshment', closely followed by Gwilym. During lunch in St Andrew's Hall, the Duke spoke of the amount of walking involved that day with the quip, 'I hope Norvic Shoes appreciate this!'

Every girl loves receiving flowers and for Joyce there was no shortage of blooms. Almost every engagement found her returning to Normandie Tower with a colourful bouquet. But Joyce had no intention of keeping these to herself, either placing them in the communal living area or knocking on a door and presenting them to an astonished neighbour. Over twelve months, Joyce undertook 663 official meetings and receptions, ate 122 meals and made a total of ninety-six speeches. She went to church twenty-four times, wore both the red and the black and gold robes thirty-one times each and donned her chain of office 307 times.[10] The press dubbed her 'the most photographed Lord Mayor'. On Tuesday, 19 May 1976, her loyal neighbours joined hundreds of other city residents, lining the length of Rouen Road two or three deep, to applaud and wave as the civic coach, drawn by two dappled shire horses, took Joyce, Gwilym and granddaughter Selina – a princess in a blue dress for the day – from Normandie Tower to the steps of City Hall, where Joyce was to transfer the ancient chain of office to the incoming Lord Mayor, Raymond Frostick. The fairy tale was over.

Joyce stood down as a councillor in 1979, after seventeen years' service to the city, although it was not her intention to slow down. Referring to her work with Norwich Area Health Authority, she said, 'I shall be able to spend more time visiting the hospitals and the ambulance stations.' Other ongoing responsibilities included two decades of chairing the Charing Cross Centre, a popular community amenity in the city, setting up a charity shop and café, with Selina helping on the till on Saturdays. Always busy, Joyce was actively involved with the Norfolk and Norwich Pensioners Association and with Norwich City College as a governor. An energetic campaigner for good causes, Joyce would often be seen brandishing a placard at public demonstrations. Four years before standing down from the Council, she was made a trustee of Age Concern Norwich, becoming its chairman in 1984 and being appointed Life President on her retirement ten years later. Gwilym found himself fending for himself much of the time, but when she was home Joyce dutifully looked after his every need. As his health began to fail, Joyce nursed him with devotion, losing him to cancer in April 1993, just six weeks before their golden wedding anniversary.

In February 1994, Joyce was introduced to one of the Age Concern new volunteers. Bill Knight had lost his wife Gill only a few months earlier and was quite alone, with no children or close relatives. Her heart melting, Joyce took him dancing, discovering Bill to be hopeless on the dance floor. Joyce was living in a council flat next door to her brother Terry in Lothian Street. Every morning, Bill would drive from his four-bedroomed home in affluent Cringleford to share the day with Joyce, always returning home at 9.00 pm. They enjoyed many trips and holidays together, including a number of cruises. Bill always maintained that Joyce saved him from a lonely old age. He shared her delight when Selina married in 1994 and her disappointment when the young couple moved to Somerset. They were both thrilled to become great-grandparents to Charlotte, born in 1999, and Eleanor, born in 2002.

During this period, Bill was diagnosed with prostate cancer. In order to nurse him properly, Joyce suggested they move in together permanently, but insisted on marrying first. Bill did not hesitate, contacting the registrar and booking a June wedding in 2001. However, in 2003 their happiness was put on hold when Joyce's only son, John, was diagnosed with Non-Hodgkin's lymphoma, an aggressive cancer of the lymphatic system. John, since divorced from Sandra and now married to Denise, died at the James Paget Hospital in Great Yarmouth, aged fifty-nine.

Despite Bill supporting both Joyce and Denise through their intense grief, Joyce suffered a breakdown some months later, leading to a stay in hospital. Bill also had deteriorating health issues, losing the fight in February 2011. Joyce thought of him every day to the end of her life, coming on 24 November 2012 at the Priscilla Bacon Lodge Hospice in the Unthank Road after some years of battling angina and a progressive cancer. Selina inherited boxes of civic memorabilia, photographs and newspaper cuttings from Joyce's fifty years in public life. For Selina they remain a reminder of a magical time – the year she shared her beloved Nan with the City of Norwich.

Endnotes

1. Nine months earlier, Mrs Thatcher won an unexpected and decisive victory for the Conservative Party leadership over Edward Heath.
2. The *Eastern Evening News* reported that Mrs Thatcher was wearing a 'turquoise coat and matching neck-scarf' and stopped to admire a men's clothing stall, commenting that some items might suit her son Mark. She paused to speak with Betty Chandler at her doll and fancy goods stall.
3. Terry Bird, speaking in 2016.
4. That same night, raids took place in historic towns such as Bath, Canterbury, Exeter and York. They became known as the Baedeker Raids, after the famous guidebooks, assuming that the Nazi Luftwaffe selected the cultural centres in retaliation for the British bombing of Lübeck on 28 March 1942.
5. www.georgeplunkett.co.uk/Website/raids.htm
6. Scrivens, P., *Escaping Hitler: A Jewish Boy's Quest for Freedom and His Future*, Pen & Sword, Barnsley, 2016.
7. *Eastern Evening News*, 20 May 1975.
8. Joe Stirling was the first Sheriff of Norwich to be recruited from outside the ranks of sitting councillors, following the local government reorganisation of 1974.
9. Lord Mayor of Norwich 1986–87.
10. Rennie, Jean, 'Portrait of a Lady', *Norfolk Fair Magazine*, September 1976.

Joyce Lilian Morgan 1975–76

Further Highlights from her Mayoral Year

- Shaking more than 700 hands as she and Gwilym welcomed delegates to a Conference of the British Pharmaceutical Society at St Andrew's Hall.

- Returning, at the invitation of the station commander, to RAF Marham as Lord Mayor, in a chauffeur-driven limousine bearing the civic crest. She had left there thirty-two years earlier as WAAF Corporal Joyce Bird.

- Greeting a group of German students from Heidelberg on an exchange visit with Norwich High School for Girls. Presenting them with a plaque to stress the importance of twinning with cities and schools.

- Enjoying a cheese and wine buffet party hosted by the Norwich Footwear Manufacturer's Association, in the crypt of St Andrew's Hall at the end of Norwich Shoe Week.

- Receiving a bouquet from a circus performer at Robert Fossett's Big Top, having watched, alongside twenty councillors, a show featuring elephants, camels, llamas and Bobo the Clown.

- Greeting Lieutenant Rob Farmer of HMS *Norfolk* as he entered Norwich on a Penny Farthing bicycle, at the head of a group completing a sponsored cycle from Newcastle to Norwich.

- Flying from Norwich on a scheduled Air Anglia flight to Bergen in Norway, the most northern point served by the airline, where she and Gwilym met the Mayor of Bergen.

- Receiving a Waterford Crystal vase from the standing committee of Norwich Women's Organisations in honour of International Women's Year.

- Spending the week leading up to Christmas visiting patients in hospitals all over Norwich, distributing gifts, singing carols and spreading festive cheer.

- Conferring the Freedom of the City of Norwich onto 24-year-old printer Andrew King, on the same day as his wedding in North Walsham.

CHAPTER 6

Valerie Guttsman (1918–2009)

Lord Mayor of Norwich 1979–80

It's very difficult to say what my native language is. My mother mainly spoke Hungarian, my father mainly German, and at school it was all Slovak. I probably mainly spoke Hungarian but all our maids were Slovak and when we were sitting together having a meal as a family, we drifted from one language into another without even noticing, according to the subject we were discussing.

(Valerie Guttsman, in conversation with Dr Julie Charlesworth, June 1998)

In 1962, German born Willi Guttsman, his Czech wife Valerie and their only child, 4-year-old Janet, moved to Norwich from London. As the couple set up home, neither of them could have imagined the influence they would have on this East Anglian city.

Valerie Lichtigova was born on 3 June 1918 to Jewish parents, the youngest of four daughters. The family home was the tiny village of Hatalov, at the time of her birth located in Austria-Hungary; four months later, the Empire collapsed with the creation of the independent First Republic of Czechoslovakia. While Valerie was still a baby, the family moved to the university town of Prešov. Her father was a travelling wine merchant; her mother read biographies and loved researching local history. Much of the housework, gardening and childcare was left to the servants. During long winter evenings, Valerie, Adele, Olga and Ella sat entranced as the maid told frightening folk tales of murder and magic while skilfully stripping goose feathers for eiderdowns. With no less than sixty-two first cousins, the girls were never short of companions, the Lichtigova sisters each visiting their favourites during the summer and enjoying holidays full of swimming, singing and laughter.

Compulsory education began at six years old, with classes of forty or fifty children – the consequence of a post-war baby boom. There was no time for individual attention; pupils chanted their lessons by rote. Short-sighted from an early age, young Valerie sat on the front row. Discipline was strict. Separated from her sisters and sent to the academic Protestant secondary school, Valerie's diminutive stature and poor vision left her vulnerable to bullying. Despite this, she left school with excellent grades and applied to read Medicine at Prague University, the family moving to the city once Adele had left home for a future in Palestine. But political tensions were deepening. Places at the university were limited and Valerie reluctantly transferred to read Chemistry. On 15 March 1939, Nazi troops invaded Czechoslovakia, establishing a protectorate over Bohemia and Moravia. Valerie was now categorised as a foreigner. By chance she met with five young Jewish men, recently escaped from Nazi Germany, each with a coveted visa for England. They taught her how to bribe the right people, and within four days she had her papers. Valerie boarded a train with her new friends, uncertain if she would ever see her home again. By the end of the Second World War, Valerie's parents, her sisters Olga and Ella, and most of her sixty-four cousins had been murdered by the Nazis.

Valerie first found work in Glasgow, at the home of a dentist and his family, sharing a room with a young Scottish girl. Days were spent lighting fires, cleaning, ironing and sewing. The early morning chores complete, the girls changed into clean starched aprons and pretty caps, and greeted patients into the surgery. Valerie had little time to study her textbook, *English for Foreigners*. Once she had discovered that her roommate and the master were 'carrying on', Valerie gave in her notice. Her next job was on an isolated farm, just outside the village of Dunlop, 25 miles south-west of Glasgow. Her tiny attic room was above the kitchen, only accessible by stepladder. The ceiling was so low she could barely stand, and getting dressed was an acrobatic feat. Finding the toilet at night meant feeling her way between two lines of sleeping cows. Every morning her job was to empty the full churns of milk into coolers high above her head. Every Sunday, Valerie joined a group of young European refugees for an afternoon in the stunning Scottish countryside. It was during one of those gatherings that Valerie met Wilhelm Leo Guttsman, who very soon asked her to call him Willi.

Willi was born in Berlin, into a middle-class, non-observant Jewish family, on 23 August 1920. As a youth he enjoyed hiking and cycling, Expressionist painting, classical music, and reading Goethe, Schiller and Marx. In 1933, with the Nazi Party in control, Willi's father, Walter Guttsman, was dismissed from his senior engineer's job with electronics giant AEG. Two years later, short of money and concerned for their safety, the family moved permanently to their rural holiday cottage, where they grew vegetables in the cherry orchard. As the political situation worsened Hannah was sent to Palestine on a one-way ticket. On the night of Kristallnacht (Night of Broken Glass), 8–9 November 1938, Willi, now eighteen, was interned in Buchenwald, a Nazi concentration camp built originally to house political prisoners. Willi considered himself lucky when he was categorised as an ordinary German prisoner, for the Jews were kept separate, their treatment hidden from the others. After two and a half months, Willi was released and he left Germany in March 1939, his parents having secured him an exit visa. They themselves were not so fortunate. In September 1939, at the outbreak of war, they were forced to sell their Potsdam house and move back to Berlin to live with relatives. In 1941, they were deported to Majdanek Extermination Camp, where they perished.

Willi travelled to Scotland and joined a scheme whereby refugees picked potatoes for Ayrshire farmers in return for bed and board. Firmly believing he would ultimately join his sister in Palestine, he toiled on the land, biding his time. Amongst the many friends he made in Scotland, his favourite by far was the diminutive Czech milkmaid. In the spring of 1940, many refugees were reassigned, and were sent to the market gardens around St Albans in Hertfordshire. Valerie left the farm and travelled south with Willi. Following the Dunkirk evacuation, a new wave of spy fever emerged; those aliens who had been formerly considered as 'no security risk' were rounded up and interned. More than 7,000 of them, including Willi, were deported to Canada and Australia.

Willi's two-month voyage to the southern hemisphere was an ordeal. Refugees suffered humiliating treatment and violence at the hands of the crew. Before Willi left, he and Valerie vowed to wait for each other. He would be back. Valerie took a new job working on the factory floor at nearby Start-rite Shoes.[1] But she hated the deafening cacophony of machines, background music and raised voices, and soon returned to the land and relative tranquillity.

47

Within eighteen months, with his classification as an enemy alien overturned, Willi boarded the steamship *Stirling Castle*, docking in Liverpool on 28 November 1941. He and Valerie were reunited in St Albans, where he proposed marriage. For the first half of that year the couple rented a one-room furnished flat, cooking on a small trivet, carrying clean water from the landlord's bathroom, and on Saturday evenings taking a bath in 6 inches of water. No one seemed concerned that they were 'living in sin'. They became man and wife, using a borrowed ring, on 11 July 1942. The two witnesses, the only guests, joined them at a nearby coffee shop, and were asked whether they wanted coffee *or* cake, as the newlyweds couldn't afford both. It was a brief but sweet celebration. The couple led a simple life as agricultural workers, benefitting from an extra cheese ration. Sundays were spent foraging in the hedgerows, collecting stinging nettles to make the German delicacy Brennesselsuppe.

During 1943, Willi began a course of part-time study at Birkbeck College in London, his ambition to achieve a BSc in Economics. But the travelling and weekdays away from Valerie became intolerable. When a vacancy arose at the United Kingdom Search Bureau in London, an organisation locating missing Jewish refugees, he applied. Having settled into a rented flat in North London, Valerie began training as a nursery nurse. The capital proved a very different environment from peaceful leafy Hertfordshire. From January to May 1944, the south of England was subject to a 'mini-blitz', suffering sustained bombing from the German Luftwaffe in retaliation for Allied attacks on German cities. Tragically, a number of Valerie's young charges were either killed or made homeless. Her days were filled with anxious little faces, nappies and cod liver oil, her evenings spent studying for vocational qualifications. By September, a new menace had arrived in the shape of V-2 missiles. One night, as Valerie and Willi slept, they were shaken awake by a massive explosion to find themselves lying deep in rubble, timber and glass, staring up at a clear star-studded sky. At sunrise they stepped outside; every house in the street was damaged. Still in shock, they took a bus to Richmond Park and slept on the grass for the entire day.

On 7 May 1945, Germany signed an unconditional surrender. Liberated survivors of the Holocaust began arriving in London. Valerie was approached to become matron of a residential home, caring for twenty boys orphaned by the atrocities. She found the children to be profoundly disturbed from their experiences, many having witnessed the deaths of their parents. Valerie was kind yet firm, having to deal with a variety of behavioural and emotional problems. Six months later, she responded to an urgent appeal for trainee social workers; her qualifications, including one in psychiatric social work from the London School of Economics (LSE), secured her offers from Great Ormond Street Hospital for Sick Children and the National Hospital for Nervous Diseases.

Willi graduated from Birkbeck College in 1946, taking up a post as Junior Library Assistant at the LSE, working in an office deep in the basement. Despite his persisting health issues, still evident from his time in Buchenwald, Willi stoically undertook his duties while studying for an MSc in Economics. In 1948, the couple became naturalised British subjects and immediately joined the Labour Party. Although they had good jobs, many friends and a comfortable home, Willi and Valerie had one persistent disappointment: after fifteen years of trying for a baby, at thirty-nine Valerie was referred to the sub-fertility clinic at Hammersmith. Over her course of treatment she suffered no fewer than six miscarriages. Early in 1958, Valerie became pregnant again, giving birth to her daughter Janet later that year.

During the opening months of the 1960s, at Norwich City Hall an appeal committee was actively raising funds to build the new University of East Anglia. On 17 May 1962, with generous donations from wealthy individuals and businesses already in the bank, a public appeal was launched. The inaugural Vice Chancellor, Frank Thistlethwaite, a historian from the University of Cambridge, had been in place since October 1961 and was now ready to recruit two key figures – a founding librarian and a registrar. A glowing reference arrived from the LSE for one Wilhelm Guttsman, currently employed as the Acquisitions Officer and Deputy Librarian at LSE. At his interview, members of the panel found him to be 'a political sociologist of distinction'.[2] They were impressed. When could he start?

Willi set to work in the temporary surroundings of the Georgian Dining room of Earlham Hall, procuring an initial catalogue of textbooks in time for the first student intake in October 1963. Despite his immense workload, Willi successfully completed the manuscript of his first book, *The British Political Elite*,[3] which rapidly became the most frequently cited work on the topic. The dedication reads, 'For Valerie who helped and for Janet who distracted'. Valerie spent her time setting up home, identifying childcare and schools for Janet, all while desperately navigating her way around an unfamiliar city. She had a hopeless sense of direction, and even after years of living in Norwich she could still get lost within a mile of her home.

Everyone was curious to meet those elite few who would be moulding the new university and Valerie and Willi regularly received gilt-edged invitations to drinks parties and receptions. Members of the local Labour Party began gently persuading Valerie to become involved. Intrigued, Valerie swiftly became a valued activist, serving on working parties, sitting on the executive, and even speaking from the platform at local conferences. In June 1964, when the city councillor for Crome Ward was promoted to Alderman, a by-election was called and Valerie was named as the Labour candidate. When the seat was unopposed, she was automatically the victor. She and Willi took to walking around her patch looking for areas that could use some improvement.

Her confidence growing, Valerie began asking questions, picking up clues about the etiquette of meetings. Over time she gained a reputation as an erudite speaker, although a little verbose; committee chairmen allowed additional time if Councillor Guttsman was involved in a debate. She had respect for order and regulations, and was compelled to complete a task, ably addressing problems and seeking solutions. She quickly became the 'go to' councillor for anything related to children, health, the elderly and social services, and she was invited to sit on numerous committees, boards and working parties. When elected to the Labour Party National Executive, she travelled once a month to London, working closely with well-known senior politician Barbara Castle, MP for Blackburn since 1945. For ten years from 1973, Valerie held seats on both the City and the County councils. As a 'twin-hatter'[4] she worked up to sixty hours a week, sharing her time between City Hall and County Hall.

Early in 1979, Valerie was nominated as Lord Mayor of Norwich. She was sixty-one, with fifteen years' experience as a councillor. During the three-month run-up to Mayor-Making day, Valerie slept badly, resorting to sitting up in bed stitching patchwork from 5.00 am until breakfast. Willi, stoic as ever, never complained. By the morning of 15 May 1979, the hem of the black and gold robe had been taken up and a large cushion placed on the Chairman's chair in the Chamber. The new Sheriff was W. Rowan Hare, retired Chief Executive of Colman's, a major player in the establishment of UEA and a well-known 'character' renowned for walking the streets and talking to everyone, exercising his phenomenal recall for people's names. Both he and Valerie were duly inaugurated in front of a packed council chamber, including 20-year-old Janet, flown in from Birmingham, where she was studying Social Sciences at the university. For Valerie this appointment was a 'fairy tale come true'.[5] She was determined to bring people from all walks of life into her parlour, offering them the opportunity to share ideas and iron out any differences. Her first outside engagement was the traditional annual lunch held by Norwich Rotary Club, where Valerie took a direct approach, setting out a four-point plan, encouraging the assembled businessmen to help the children and young people of the city. Her efforts were rewarded when Rotarian Joe Cook immediately offered to fund a city drop-in centre and crèche on Saturday mornings. At a similar event the following year, Valerie paid tribute to Norwich, saying, 'Norwich was the first city to trust a woman to be Lord Mayor, and Norwich is now the first city to trust a foreign woman to be Lord Mayor.'[6]

When the Prince of Wales accepted an invitation to attend a charity dinner and dance in Norwich during the early summer, protocol dictated that Charles would take the first dance with the highest-ranking woman in the room. But Valerie was no dancer and City Hall informed the Palace in advance that the Lord Mayor would, with regret, be turning him down. Valerie was the first female Lord Mayor to enjoy her Lord Mayor's Procession, an annual tradition instituted in its modern format in 1976.[7] While presiding at a Freemen of Norwich[8] ceremony – only the second woman to do so[9] – daughters and sisters of recipients approached Valerie, demanding that, after many centuries, eligible women should now be given the right to become Freemen. When Valerie lobbied the all-male committee, they were unimpressed, one member responding, 'Over my dead body.'[10] It would be a further thirty years until Lord Mayor Eve Collishaw conferred the title of Freeman of Norwich on a woman for the first time. During her mayoral year, Valerie attended over 900 functions and delivered more than 400 speeches, regularly accompanied by Willi.

By May 1983, Valerie had stood down from both her county and city seats. She had faithfully served the residents of her little patch of Norwich for seventeen years. She could now devote more time to her committees and charity work. In 1985, Willi retired from the UEA, honoured with the title of Librarian Emeritus. His final art exhibition to be staged at UEA featured German political art from the 1920s, a lifelong passion. In retirement he planned to produce an illustrated volume on the role of visual art in the German working-class environment, researching in archives, museums and galleries in Germany. This project would absorb him for the rest of his life.

On 15 June 1991, Valerie's service to the community in Norwich and Norfolk was recognised at the highest level when she was made an Officer of the most Excellent Order of the British Empire (OBE). She was overwhelmed. However, plans for her and Willi's joint retirements were curtailed when her husband was diagnosed with Parkinson's disease. Determined to complete his book, Willi continued his research overseas, but his movements became progressively constrained, his voice reduced to a whisper. He persevered, and in July 1997, *Art for the Workers: Ideology and the Visual Arts in Weimar Germany* was released. Willi died on 13 February 1998. This modest man, totally unaware of the significance of his legacy, had enriched so many lives. Valerie was bereft.

Willi lived long enough to see Janet realise her dream of becoming an international journalist, working in major cities for Reuters News Agency. Some years into the new millennium, Janet took her mother on a nostalgic trip to Slovakia, calling at both Valerie's home village of Hatalov and the city of Prešov. It was not an easy journey. Several years later, having suffered two broken hips and survived months of illness, Valerie moved into Corton House, a care home for the elderly in City Road. It was here that she entered a period of mental decline. On 29 September 2009, she died peacefully, knowing that her daughter had married in America. Janet and Bruce travelled to Norwich for the funeral on 8 October, where she paid tribute to this very special woman:

> I asked my mother not very long ago why she and my father had chosen to make their lives here in England, rather than any of the other places they could have gone when the war ended. She answered me very simply: 'This was the place where we thought we could feel at home.'

Endnotes

1. Start-rite was established in 1792 by leatherworker James Smith in a small shop behind Norwich Market.
2. Sanderson, Michael, *The History of the University of East Anglia, Norwich*, Hambledon & London, London, 2002, p.113.
3. Guttsman, W.L., *The British Political Elite*, MacGibbon & Kee, London, 1964.
4. A councillor holding a seat on two different local authorities at the same time.
5. *Norwich Mercury*, 23 February 1979.

6. *Evening News*, 19 February 1980.

7. For many centuries, processions and parades were an integral part of civic life, the fun coming to an end with the Municipal Corporation Reform Act in 1835. In 1971, a proposal was put forward for the creation of 'A Grand Norwich Festival' to promote the city, the leadership coming from civic leaders. Years of planning culminated in the summer of 1976 with a 'Snap 76' festival, named after the Norwich dragon. The first procession, with Lord Mayor Richard Frostick, was themed 'Norwich Through the Ages' and over forty organisations entered floats and walking groups. It was not without incident. The Lord Mayor and Lady Mayoress were travelling in the civic coach when one of the horses was spooked by the crowd, forcing the pair to hastily disembark, crowding into the open Rolls-Royce carrying the Festival's Miss Snap, Patricia Boaden. The Lord Mayor's Procession is one of the most anticipated annual events in the city's calendar. (*Norwich – The Revival of the Lord Mayor's Procession in 1976*, by Raymond Frostick.)

8. It is 700 years since the first Freeman was recorded in the earliest Norwich Register in 1317, and in 2017 the city celebrated this anniversary. The Freemen were once the governing body of the city and granted special rights to trade freely and conduct business. The title still survives and there are currently over 1,000 Freemen of Norwich, including 400 women (first entitled to apply in 2010), most of whom are direct descendants of original freemen.

9. The first was Jessie Griffiths, 1969–70.

10. Guttsman, V., unpublished memoir lodged at Norwich Record Office.

Valerie Guttsman 1979–80

Further Highlights from her Mayoral Year

- Receiving over 300 guests to the Lord Mayor's 'At Home' event in the Castle Keep, including the Bishop of Norwich, the MP for Norwich North, and Joyce Morgan, the last woman before Valerie to hold the post of Lord Mayor.

- Attending the annual dinner of the Showmen's Guild of Great Britain, held in the Norwood Rooms, alongside the Mayors of Cambridge, Peterborough and King's Lynn.

- Flying in a private jet from Norwich Airport to Rouen, to be special guests at an historic event, the blessing of a new church, where an old stained glass window, hidden during the war, was reinstated in its rightful position. Enjoying a fly-past and spectacular dinner before leaving for Rouen airport.

- Performing the Topping Out ceremony at Norwich Job Centre while dispensing beer to the workmen.

- Celebrating the fiftieth anniversary of the National Association of Industries for the Blind and Disabled, when officially opening a national exhibition of work in Norwich Cathedral.

- Watching a private air acrobatics display by the Red Arrows at RAF Coltishall, the final opportunity to see the bright red Gnat training aircraft before they transferred to the larger Hawk the following year.

- Sitting in the cockpit of a Gnat aircraft, once flown by the Red Arrows, at the opening of the RAF Careers exhibition at St Andrew's car park.

- Being the first female to host an annual Lord Mayor's Procession in its modern format, as instituted in 1976, and judging the Best Float and Best Dressed Shop Window competitions.

- Receiving a standing ovation following a speech to 450 veterans and wives from the 2nd Air Division of the 8th US Air Force, based in Norfolk during the war.

- Standing precariously on an empty oil drum in order to pin a rosette onto a prize-winning horse!

CHAPTER 7

Barbara Ellen Edith Stevenson (1919–)

Lord Mayor of Norwich 1985–86

Arthur South had a lady who worked for him in the Norwich Fur Company who made alterations to all the robes and gowns. The main one was black and gold. I followed Stan Petersen, who was a fairly big man. I went out to see Val and when I put it on, the robe spread out like a peacock's fan! It was very difficult because the gold band of about an inch and a half has to be at the edge at the front and around the bottom. To get it in the right place it had to be turned up twice, so the gold came at the bottom. Sort of folded in the middle. And then you do the same to the corners. It was like wearing a block of wood.

(Barbara Stevenson, speaking in 2017)

In the rural Norfolk village of Bedingham, near Bungay in June 1916, farm labourer Bertie Austin Yallop had just turned eighteen. Three months previously, in a desperate effort to recruit more fighting men, the British Government passed the Military Service Act. Bertie was eligible for conscription. It was year two of the Great War. Bertie said goodbye to his widowed grandmother, Alice Yallop, who had raised him from a baby,[1] and travelled to Norwich and signed the oath of allegiance before being assigned to the Fourth East Surrey Regiment.

His sweetheart, Beatrice Ellen Hazell, known as Beattie, remained behind in her nearby home village of Hempnall with her mother Ellen and father Benjamin, a horseman on a local farm. Beattie prayed for Bertie's safe return. He was one of the few to survive the mud and the blood of the Battle of Passchendaele during 1917. Home on leave in June 1918, Bertie published the banns of marriage. For reasons that are unclear, the wedding was delayed until the end of 1919, just a few weeks before Beattie gave birth to a daughter in their home at Topcroft Mill on 19 November. The baby was very tiny, 'small enough to be bathed in a pint pot'. They called her Barbara, and for decades she was known as 'Little Bee'.

Over the next four years the couple had three more daughters: Olive, Ivy and Marjorie, the youngest, born in March 1934. Bertie suffered bouts of debilitating asthma, a result of inhaling gas during the war, and this limited his ability to work. He supported his family as a local postman, also turning his hand to boot and shoe repairing. He progressed to saddler, making reins and other leather goods. Bertie was a God-fearing man, a regular worshipper and church warden. Beattie was too busy to go to church. The family kept a modest smallholding, growing vegetables and keeping cows, pigs and donkeys. Like most of rural Norfolk at that time, their home had no electricity, gas or flush toilet. Fresh water was from the pump outside the back door and boiling a kettle meant lighting a fire.

When Barbara was nine years old, the Equal Franchise Act of 1928 gave women over twenty-one the right to vote. Women were already playing their part on Norwich Borough Council. Mabel Clarkson was elected in 1913 as a Liberal councillor, and in 1923, Ethel Colman became the first female Lord Mayor of Norwich, and indeed the first in the UK. In 1930, when Barbara was travelling by bus to the Blyth School for Girls in the city, Mabel Clarkson became the second female Lord Mayor. At this time, Dorothy Jewson, one of the first three Labour women MPs elected to Parliament, was also an active Norwich councillor. These women were inspirational to the young Barbara, who was already demonstrating a lively and enquiring mind.

For many women at that time, the Independent Labour Party (ILP), founded in 1893, with its historical links to the suffragette movement, seemed a natural home. During Easter 1915, Keir Hardie, a founding father of the Labour movement, famously spoke against the war in his last public speech, during the ILP annual conference in Norwich. By September he was dead, and the hall in St Gregory's Alley was renamed in his honour in 1916. During the 1940s, the building became the home of Norwich Working Men's Club, remaining a popular social venue until its closure in 2014. As a young school leaver, it was in this hall that Barbara discovered the social side of the ILP, travelling home to Bedingham on the last bus at 9.30 pm. It was here that she met a young communist sympathiser, Len Stevenson. They must have turned heads, with Barbara standing at only 4 feet 11 inches and Len just under 6 feet. They enjoyed talking to each other and before long Barbara found herself joining the Communist Party to be near Len. She remembers, 'I thought it would be simpler if we were both in the same party. But I couldn't take the discipline.' A year later she did not renew her membership.

With the onset of the Second World War, Len joined the RAF as ground crew, stationed both at Halesworth and Great Yarmouth. He hated flying. With Len being only twenty, and Barbara twenty-one, the couple were doubtful that Len would get permission from his parents to marry, so they went ahead regardless and the wedding was held in June 1941. With Len away, Barbara lived with his parents on Cadge Road, to the west of the city, and she worked in an insurance office. In the evenings she would sometimes join her father-in-law, a full-time firewatcher, standing on roofs and helping where she could. Once the conflict was over, Len and Barbara set up home together in Norwich.

On 5 July 1948, the Labour government launched the National Health Service. Five months later, on Boxing Day 1948, Barbara benefitted from its 'free services for all at the point of delivery' when she was admitted to Earlham Hall Maternity Hospital. After two long days in labour, the staff decided to try the preferred method of inducing birth: castor oil floating in orange juice followed by a hot drink and an even hotter bath! Initially this failed. A day later, well into contractions, Barbara suffered convulsions, which were diagnosed as eclampsia due to rapidly rising blood pressure. A sickly baby Anya emerged on 29 December. Medics were concerned for the survival of both mother and baby, and Len must have feared he would lose his whole world.

Barbara and Len were advised not to have any more babies for the time being, but only sixteen months later, their son Julian was born. This time the birth was relatively straightforward. At three years old Julian became obsessed with the neighbours' newborn. He wanted one of his own, mithering his mother until she enquired about fostering a child. Barbara still recalls the rigmarole required to complete the application:

> You had to promise to take the child to church and enrol them and your own children into Sunday school. My doctor and the woman

in charge of the Mother and Baby Clinic provided references. The Chairman of the Foster Committee said, 'With references that good we couldn't turn you down even if we wanted to!'

Within a few weeks, Barbara and Len took charge of Trevor, a 5-month-old baby whose mother was suffering from tuberculosis and struggling to care for her four boys under five. Julian loved his present but Trevor was not with the Stevenson family long as his mother discharged herself from hospital and claimed her boys back. Barbara had become fond of the child, but saw him again on only one occasion. With Christmas approaching, Barbara had taken a job in the General Post Office canteen, travelling there by bus. One day, Trevor's mum boarded the bus with the baby in her arms. He was wearing a coat that Barbara had made for Anya when she was small. He looked unwell and it broke Barbara's heart to see him. Len went to Trevor's home to present him with a wooden train set as a Christmas gift and was shocked and saddened by the poor state in which the family lived. Although the authorities later asked Barbara to foster baby twins, she was disheartened and said no. Barbara and Len did not take in a child again.[2]

A family friend, Dick Seabrook, offered Barbara a full-time job as clerk to the organiser in the Norwich office of the Union of Shop, Distributive and Allied Workers (USDAW). Dick would travel to London to negotiate with management teams, principally in the food manufacturing industry, calling Barbara at about 5.00 pm to instruct her to produce a circular to be sent out immediately to shop stewards outlining the results of his delicate negotiations. Barbara's job and her political interests began to overlap and soon became inseparable. Len was in a similar position. For many years he was the office manager at the Norwich furnishing store Taskers of Fishergate. Despite this, in the May elections of 1953 Len stood as the Communist Party candidate for Earlham Ward. After his defeat he concluded his best chance of being elected was to transfer his allegiance to Labour. Initially he faced some resistance from the older councillors and activists, who had encountered Len's intransigence and sharp tongue on many occasions. Barbara not only supported her husband in his ambition, but also later joined him, first standing as a city councillor in 1958, losing in Mancroft Ward by only eighty-two votes. In the same year the family moved into a much larger council house in the historic Elm Hill.

Undeterred by election defeats, they both stood again in 1959, Len winning a seat for Labour in Lakenham, and Barbara standing in

Town Close. During her campaign, Barbara became renowned for her rousing speeches, lauding recent Labour successes – the completion of the South Tuckswood Shopping Centre, Harford Hall Playing Fields and the rehousing of former slum dwellers into new flats in Victoria Street. She lost the seat, but in June 1961 she was able to join Len on the Council when she won a by-election in Catton Ward, which had been called when Arthur South, Labour Leader of the City Council, was elected as an alderman and consequently resigned his seat.

Both Len and Barbara quickly established themselves at City Hall. Len chaired planning, housing and property committees and was a droll speaker, outspoken and well read, with an incredible facility to retain facts. It was said that his weekly meetings with the Chief Officer drew heavily on whisky, kept in his drinks cupboard. Once, when showing a Russian guest around the Planning Department, Len was asked how many people worked there. He replied, 'At any one time about half of them!' Vocal and stubborn, he was often confrontational in the Chamber; unlike his wife who, although an equally determined and strong character, tended to be more considered, speaking knowledgeably on issues close to her heart. She was an effective councillor, being as equally conscientious as when a school governor or sitting on the National Health Service Executive Council, or, from 1971, on the Eastern Gas Consumers' Council. Barbara's view was that Len 'looked after things' whilst she 'looked after people'.

With Norwich City Council holding elections every year there was always a campaign to organise. Barbara preferred to work behind the scenes, directing her troops from the safety of the committee room – usually someone's home or a church hall. While dishing out instructions, demanding updates, supervising members of the Labour Party Ladies' Section and called upon to provide catering, she would knit. Barbara was always knitting.[3] In 1967 she lost her Catton seat but persevered, returning to her old ward in 1971. Never idle, Barbara found more time for her role as full-time official at USDAW and to pursue her passions of tapestry, crochet, needlework and creating clothes for all the family.

In 1978, Len succeeded Sir Arthur South as Leader of the Council. He retired from Taskers in 1982, with Barbara leaving USDAW in February 1983. She had worked for the union for thirty years, concluding her career as Area Organiser, an unusual role for a woman, despite many of the 4,000 members being female. Leaving work enabled Len to accept the position of Lord Mayor from 1983–84. His term of office was not without controversy. A man of principal, Len's strong opposition to private medical care led him to boycott a civic visit to the new BUPA hospital at Colney. He also travelled to London to deliver a petition to Downing Street, protesting against rate capping legislation.[4] In her early retirement, Barbara kept herself busy as the Vice Chairman of the Citizen's Advice Bureau, Chairman of the Governors at Blyth-Jex School and catching up with her rug making, all while dutifully carrying out her role as Lady Mayoress.

The newspapers announced Barbara's nomination as Lord Mayor in February 1985, when she was sixty-five, the papers referring to her as a 'veteran Labour councillor'.[5] Barbara considered offering Anya the opportunity of being her official consort, but with her daughter living and working in Great Yarmouth it was deemed impractical. Len would escort her to events. At her Mayor-Making on 21 May, she paid tribute to her 87-year-old mother, three sisters, Julian, and Anya, and was accompanied by Anya's two young sons, Gavin and Jonathan. Everyone was in the Chamber to share Grandma's special day. Barbara pledged to give civic recognition to the smaller charitable organisations in the city and hoped to be remembered as the Lord Mayor who made the shortest speeches, before referring to her ongoing 'one-woman anti-fly posting campaign'.

The boom in live gigs by youth bands in the city had led to an unacceptable number of posters stuck to lampposts, traffic signs and shop windows. This became an obsession with Barbara and she frequently raised the issue at planning meetings. She made it her mission to go out after dark, often accompanied by Julian's wife, to remove the offensive notices and dispose of them in litter bins. Students from the Blyth School were drafted in to help, and even when out walking with Len she remained vigilant. Len later remarked to friends, 'I walk ahead and pretend I'm not with her.'[6]

Barbara's Sheriff was teacher and historian Geoffrey Goreham. Following his year in office he wrote and published a book about his experiences, which included some wry observations about the highs and lows of civic life.[7] With little in common, either socially or politically, the relationship between Barbara and Geoffrey was not an easy one. Barbara began her tenure by calling a meeting to 'iron out any problems'. She took her political responsibilities very seriously, particularly when chairing full council meetings, but felt relaxed around the Council staff, whether when being driven in the comfortable black Daimler by chauffeur Bill Cutting or sharing a joke with her sword and macebearers, Peter Thorpe and Stanley Taylor. She knew when the enthusiastic Stanley was on duty because of the exceptional shine on the mayoral chain and regalia.[8]

Towards the end of her mayoral year, in April 1985, Barbara had the honour of greeting Her Majesty the Queen and the Duke of Edinburgh, celebrating the twentieth anniversary of the opening of Her Majesty's Stationery Office in Anglia Square. Lord Mayor and Sheriff awaited the arrival of the Royal car, which was running late. The press pack became restless, distracting themselves by photographing perching sparrows. The Lord Lieutenant, Sir Timothy Colman, had gone to meet the Royal party at Norwich Airport, to find the plane had been delayed. On the drive back into the city, protocol dictated that Sir Timothy was to follow behind the Queen's car, making it awkward for him to introduce the Lord Mayor of Norwich to Her Majesty, as detailed on the strict programme of events. On arrival at the HMSO, well ahead of Sir Timothy, the Queen walked up the steps alone. Barbara was a little nonplussed and nervously addressed the Queen: 'I think we are meant to wait for the Lord Lieutenant, Ma'am'. The Queen smiled, telling Barbara she just wanted to say hello to the Lord Mayor. Barbara relaxed and fulfilled her civic duty by declaring confidently, 'Welcome to Norwich Your Majesty.'

Two years later, in 1988, Len became Sheriff of Norwich, in the same year as their son Julian and his wife presented the couple with twin granddaughters, Alexandra and Victoria. In 1990, Barbara retired as a councillor after nearly thirty years of devoted service, receiving her certificate of appreciation from Lord Mayor David Fullman.[9] She was seventy-one years old, and with her eyesight beginning to give real problems, it was time to stop. Sadly, Barbara's sight continued to deteriorate and despite treatment for glaucoma and cataracts, she was eventually diagnosed with macular degeneration and registered as blind in the early 2000s.

Len too was experiencing health issues, suffering a number of heart attacks, and by early 2007 showing early signs of dementia. He was admitted to the Julian Hospital, where tragically he developed an infection and was transferred to the Norwich and Norfolk Hospital. One afternoon in March, having paid Len a visit, Barbara remarked to Anya, 'I don't think we'll see him alive again.' This proved prophetic when Len died that same evening. When a 'civic' passes away, the tradition is for councillors past and present, many former Lord Mayors and Sheriffs, to attend the funeral. Len's was no exception. The crematorium was full.

Barbara continues to live quietly in sheltered housing in Union Street, Norwich. Of the Yallop sisters, only she and Marjorie survive.[10] In 2013, at only sixty-six, Barbara's son Julian died suddenly, just three weeks after walking his daughter Victoria down the aisle. The family still feels his loss. But Barbara continues to enjoy regular visits from Anya, hearing news of her four grandchildren. At ninety-eight years old she is as determined as ever, her ambition to live long enough to receive that very special birthday telegram from the Queen.

Endnotes

1. Family legend and genealogy research suggests that Bertie's mother was Alice Anna Yallop, second daughter of William and Alice Yallop from Bedingham. Sadly, in 1891, when Alice Anna was ten years old, her father died, aged forty-two. He left a widow and five children. Alice Anna went to work as a maid in a nearby vicarage, falling pregnant aged seventeen after an alleged assignation with either the clergyman or his son. Alice Anna left the baby, Bertie Austin, in the care of her mother, leaving home to take up another position in service and later marrying.

2. In March 2017, the author searched for Trevor in a bid to connect him and Barbara after several decades. With the help of Facebook, Trevor was found, living near Melbourne in Australia and working from home as an independent consultant. He had been married forty-two years, with two children, the first born in Norwich, and four grandchildren. Barbara and Anya were delighted to learn of his success.

3. Barbara recalls knitting at the back of the USADW conference in the Winter Gardens, Blackpool, when she dropped her ball of wool, watching it roll right to the front. Unperturbed, she broke off the twine, and started again with a fresh ball.

4. Obituary for Len Stevenson, *Evening News*, March 2007.

5. *Evening News*, 22 February 1985.

6. *Evening News*, 17 May 1985.

7. Goreham, Geoffrey, *The Sheriff's Tale*, Crowes of Norwich, 1986.

8. After London, Norwich is said to have the finest collection of civic regalia of any city in the country. In the past the priceless swords, maces and plate were stored first in the Guildhall, then City Hall, and now in Norwich Castle, where they are on public display. In the Middle Ages, the swords and maces were meant as weapons, carried before a king in order to protect him. Today they are held by uniformed mace bearers at formal civic occasions such as Mayor-Making and the Civic Service held at Norwich Cathedral. These include the Howard Mace, given to the city by Lord Henry Howard on the occasion of a visit by Charles II in 1671, and

the Walpole Mace, given to the city by Sir Robert Walpole, Britain's first prime minister. The civic sword was presented by Nelson and is a relic of the battle of Cape St Vincent in 1797, and was featured in a portrait of the Admiral by Sir William Beechy in 1801.

9. David Fullman became the Lord Mayor of Norwich for the second time in May 2017.
10. As at June 2017.

Lord Mayor Barbara Stevenson 1985–86

Further Highlights from her Mayoral Year

- Welcoming guests to her 'At Home' reception at Norwich Castle Museum, eating nuts and sausage rolls while becoming accustomed to the weight of the mayoral chain.

- Touring the Colman factory at Carrow and talking with employees.

- Spooning strawberries and cream from long glasses at an Edwardian 'At Home', hosted by the High Sheriff of Norwich, Sir Jeffrey Darnell. Listening to the tunes from *My Fair Lady* played by a band on a covered stand.

- Processing with academics and Norfolk civic leaders at the University of East Anglia before witnessing students receiving their degrees from the newly elected chancellor.

- Riding in a white Rolls-Royce ahead of the civic blue bus and more than ninety floats in the Lord Mayor's Procession, and waving to a crowd of 40,000, having first been wined and dined at The Strangers' Club in Elm Hill. Watching the firework display from Bethel Street car park.

- Standing in a fourteenth-century undercroft in King Street, while opening a restoration project by Norwich Preservation Trust.

- Being presented by the developers with the trowel she used to put the final touches to the Cavendish Court Housing Scheme.

- Taking lunch in the beautiful Marble Hall at the Norwich Union offices in Surrey Street.

- Steaming upriver in an Edwardian boat, following a procession of craft led by 'Queen Elizabeth' in costume at the Cow Tower Fete.

- Taking the salute at a Freedom Parade for the Royal Anglian Regiment.

- Visiting HMS *Victory* in Portsmouth with Molly Clare. Being told to 'Mind your head, Lord Mayor' as she boarded the ship and laughing as, at her height, the instruction was quite unnecessary.

- Greeting the Duke of Kent at an art exhibition at the Assembly House and Princess Alexandra at the YMCA.

- Visiting twenty-two homes for the elderly before Christmas. Wearing the red robes and consequently being asked repeatedly if she was 'Father Christmas'!

CHAPTER 8

Jill Betty Miller
(1940–)
Lord Mayor of Norwich 1986–87

Some people come in and say 'Good morning Ma'am' and curtsey or bow, just for a laugh. Other people say, 'I suppose this will cost me double now', but it's all done in fun and with great respect. What does client Margaret Pitcher think of having her curlers fitted by the holder of one of the most ancient titles in the country? 'It's more like an honour, really. It makes you feel right proud to think that the Lord Mayor is doing your hair for you.'

(*Evening News*, 1 August 1986)

Jill Miller is a record holder. She is the only person in Norwich to have held the offices of Lord Mayor once and Sheriff twice. During each year as Sheriff she gained a grandchild. Rather more controversially, Jill was also the first Lord Mayor to commandeer the civic Daimler as a wedding car on 9 May 1987, on the occasion of the marriage of daughter Kim (an Inland Revenue administrator and talented club organist). Not everyone in the city was happy with the news, prompting several 'letters to the editor'. One particular correspondent, Mr Cox, questioned why ratepayers should pay the running costs and wages of the chauffeur for a family occasion. Two days later, the *Evening News* published a response from a D.J. Powell, resolutely defending the Lord Mayor and accusing Mr Cox of being mean spirited. 'Anyone who has attended these functions will know that Mrs Miller has carried out her duties in a charming, friendly and approachable manner. ... I feel there will be very few people who will begrudge her the use of the official car for an hour or so ... on one very important private occasion.'

In 1940, parents-to-be Herbert and Kate Steward (née Doughty) could never have imagined their new baby causing such public debate. On 9 July, in her seventh month of pregnancy, Kate feared for the future as Luftwaffe incendiary bombs fell on Boulton & Paul's Riverside Works and Carrow Hill, with 40 feet of the Old City Wall blown away. Tragically, the raid came just as Colman's employees were leaving work for the day and, with no air raid warning, twenty-six people were killed.[1] Jill Betty was born into this world at war on 23 October. Her father had been a war baby; now he had one of his own. Facing shortages, uncertainty and fear, it was a challenging time to bring up a young family.

Herbert and Kate, both Norwich born and bred, lived in St Phillips Road, a residential street of terraced houses off Dereham Road. They married in the summer of 1938, when Herbert was twenty-three. A year later, he joined up as a private in the British Army. After the birth of his daughter, Herbert was captured by the German Army, spending the remainder of his war in a German stalag. On his return home his wife could barely recognise him; he was just a bag of bones. Once recovered, Herbert returned to his trade as a brewer, working for Youngs & Crawshay in King Street, one of the four major breweries in Norwich.

Jill was an only child, attending the Avenue Road School before moving to the Model School for Girls in Dereham Road.[2] At fourteen, Jill's mother arranged for her to work on Saturdays at Mrs Gramdon's hairdressing salon, sweeping the floor and making the tea. Jill was happy with the arrangement, glad of the two shillings in her pocket at the end of the day. She began putting in a few hours after school and enrolled on some styling courses. However, on leaving school at fifteen, Jill was tempted by the wages offered at Lamberts, a well-known confectioners and tobacconists in the city, but she missed the conversations with the salon clients.

During that time, one of Jill's friends confessed to a liking for a young bus conductor and asked Jill to go with her for their first meeting. Brian Miller was much more interested in Jill, snatching her library book and asking for her address so he might return it. Not wishing to upset her girlfriend, Jill refused. The lad flirtatiously replied: 'Then I will find your house and bring the book back.' Brian and Jill were married in St Phillip's Church on 2 April 1960, the bride just twenty. The couple moved into a modest house in Heigham Street, where Jill hatched an ambitious plan. She could take a few training courses, gain some qualifications and change the back bedroom into a terrific little salon. With determination and spirit Jill soon achieved her aim, the business benefitting by being close to a number of major city manufacturing companies such as Harmers Clothing and Start-rite. Jill's client list was predominantly made up of factory workers, who dropped into 'Gillian's'[3] after work for a shampoo and set or permanent wave, sharing problems with the approachable Jill as she worked her magic on their locks. Perhaps inspired by his wife's entrepreneurial spirit, Brian resigned from the buses and opened a toy stall on Norwich Market, braving early starts and the bitter winter wind, selling jigsaws, Matchbox cars and greetings cards.

On 8 April 1966, after many years of hoping, Jill gave birth to a baby girl. Kim would be their only child. The salon walls were covered in pink congratulations cards. A regular client was Joyce Morgan,[4] Labour Councillor for Bowthorpe since 1962. Once she and Jill had covered the usual 'salon gossip', their discussions turned to politics and local issues that concerned Jill's 'ladies'. She was persuaded to help deliver Labour campaign literature door to door, especially at election time. By the early 1970s, with Joyce now a magistrate, Jill became involved in a campaign to save the nearby children's play area, a space much enjoyed by little Kim. Jill was voted spokesman for the group of concerned parents who were jubilant when, during a public meeting, Jill boldly accused the Chairman of being 'wooden'. They won the battle. The piece of land under threat was divided to include both a Scout hut and a new playground. As close friends, Jill was invited to Joyce's Mayor-Making ceremony in 1975, the hairstylist unaware that eleven years later she would be invested with the same chain of office.

Once Kim was at Nelson Street School Jill became involved in fundraising and campaigning for a school swimming pool. She was quickly becoming known as an effective activist. Early in 1979, Joyce finally persuaded Jill to stand for a City Council seat in her home ward of Heigham. Brian, now working in the Medical and Stores Department of Norfolk and Norwich Hospital, dutifully helped his wife during the campaign, leafleting, canvassing and standing on doorsteps, listening to the residents' concerns and taking notes. This was far more important than 'salon gossip'. The vote was counted in City Hall on the same night as Conservative Margaret Thatcher became the first female prime minister of the UK. The national result was a disappointment for Jill and her colleagues but they could console themselves that the Labour group was once again in control of Norwich City Council. Rookie Councillor Jill Miller was visibly excited by her new position, especially when the leader assigned her to the committees dealing with housing and environmental health, two of her particular interests. She was a 'hands-on' person, frustrated by meetings when they deteriorated into a 'talking shop'. Jill just wanted to get things done.

Jill joined a strong and experienced team of Labour women at City Hall, including Brenda Ferris,[5] Barbara Stevenson[6] and Valerie Guttsman.[7] At the suggestion of Council Leader Patricia Hollis,[8] a new Welfare Sub-Committee was established, with Jill as Chairman. This enabled her to launch major projects in the city's sheltered housing units. She led the charge to install a new, potentially lifesaving, centralised alarm system into the home of every elderly person in the city. Jill and her team actively researched what type of similar support was offered to other authority residents, visiting towns and cities outside of Norwich. It was a proud day when the first system was fitted. Jill felt gratified some time later when a survey report from the Consumer Association awarded a top rating to the system adopted by Norwich. By the early 1990s, nearly 10,000 homes in the city had a press-button emergency alarm system.

In 1983, Jill was made Deputy Lord Mayor, serving with Lord Mayor Len Stevenson. Remaining true to their convictions, the three 'civics', Len, Jill and the Sheriff of Norwich, Norman Lake, refused to attend the opening of the new BUPA Hospital in Colney on the principle that, as socialists, they did not agree with private health care.[9] In the same year, Jill remained calm when attending a reception for American servicemen as one wit called to her, 'We're right behind you Mrs Thatcher!' Jill's year as Deputy Lord Mayor proved an excellent training ground, for two years later she was nominated as Lord Mayor. Once the decision was made public, Jill was overwhelmed to receive a deluge of cards, bouquets and personal notes of congratulation. It was the first time that Norwich had honoured two women in as many years. For the past twelve months, Jill had washed and set Lord Mayor Barbara Stevenson's hair before each big occasion. Now Jill was taking her place as First Citizen. The two assistant stylists, Glenda Neal[10] and Jean Ward, could see no problem in attending to the new Lord Mayor!

Right from the start Jill was determined that the role would not change her in any way:

Lord Mayor is such an important position, and it's an honour to be chosen to represent the city, but I don't see that it makes me personally more important. Some people put on airs and graces, but I'm not made that way. I enjoy my work. I do an honest day's work, the way I have done for twenty years, and the only thing I change when I go out is my clothes. People have to accept me the way I am.[11]

Jill was equally determined to never turn down any invitation, except for unavoidable diary clashes, intending to enjoy every function, explaining: 'If you go to even a small thing, to the people there it is a big thing and there's nothing worse than someone sitting there with a long face.' Not that Jill intended giving up her business for twelve months. She would spend the time swapping her apron for a red or black robe and back again, juggling the diaries so as not to let down her regulars. Very soon a card was tucked behind a mirror in the salon. On one side it read, 'Jill In', and on the reverse, 'The Lord Mayor is Out'.[12]

As a local girl with a Norwich accent and a wide circle of friends, the press dubbed Jill 'The People's Lord Mayor'. Her Sheriff was Arthur Clare, a well-known figure in Norwich since moving from Barnet in 1954. Arthur had replaced former Kindertransport refugee Joe Stirling[13] as Agent for the Central Norfolk Labour Party before standing himself for City Council. He became known as one of the two Arthurs,[14] together dominating city politics throughout the 1960s and 1970s. Arthur's appointment meant Jill spending time with his second wife, the glamorous and feisty Zaharat Power-Clare.[15] Originally from Pakistan, she had been married to Arthur since 1979, and her exotic wardrobe and extravagant jewellery brought a flash of colour to the corridors of City Hall. It was rumoured that she owned over 200 saris and was known to be strong willed. The mayoral year was never going to be dull.

During her speech at the Mayor-Making banquet lunch, held in City Hall and watched proudly by her husband and Kim (now twenty), Jill announced her plan for the civic year. She would support a local initiative appealing to companies to 'Give a Youngster a Job'; she pledged her support to St Martins Housing Trust, providing shelter and food to the county's homeless; and publicly accepted the role of president of the recently established Norwich Alzheimer's Disease Society. The lunch was not without controversy, with councillors from the Conservative group – reduced to only four councillors at the recent council elections – losing their usual place at the top table. They had been ousted by the SDP Liberal Alliance group,[16] who boasted six councillors, under the leadership of Phillip Moore.

For the traditional Thursday evening 'At Home' reception, held in Norwich Castle, with black tie *de rigueur*, Jill wore a long dress in shades of green, her Lord Mayor's medal hanging on a silk ribbon. She positively shone as she greeted guests from all areas of Norwich life. A keen amateur photographer, Brian was busy recording every moment for the family album. As an astute businesswoman, Jill was aware of the value of this annual event, mixing with the city's employers, promoting the benefits of East Anglia and especially of Norwich.

The pace was relentless, with Jill attending more than 800 engagements over the year, sometimes up to six in one day. Everyone admired her enthusiasm, her capacity for hard work and the fact that her hair always looked good! An accomplished and keen cook, she insisted on providing buffet food for receptions held in the Lord Mayor's Parlour, spending much of the previous day alongside her mother, rustling up quiches and vol-au-vents. Kate, now over seventy, stood for hours, happily creating hundreds of homemade sausage rolls. Herbert spent the year, and many years afterwards, proudly collecting newspaper cuttings about his little girl, pasting them into paper scrapbooks for posterity.

Loyal royalist Jill had the personal pleasure of welcoming members of the Royal Family to Norwich on more than one occasion. In late May, Jill was on hand when Princess Margaret opened a £1.3 million cancer unit at the Norfolk and Norwich Hospital. In July she was alongside the Lord Lieutenant of Norfolk as Her Majesty the Queen and Prince Phillip arrived at the Royal Norfolk Show, the first time Queen Elizabeth II had attended this annual event. Wearing vivid red, the Queen and her husband rode through the Costessey site in a spectacular horse-drawn carriage procession, with striking grey horses mounted by red-coated riders complete with black silk top hats. It was the perfect day, with a record attendance, blessed with bright sunshine.

The same could not be said for Jill's Lord Mayor's procession in July. The day was one of steady cold drizzle. Civic staff suggested they close the roof of her open car, but Jill wanted to be seen and refused the offer. Coloured dye leaked from the crêpe paper decorations on many of the floats, drizzling over the tarmac, and Brian's best suit was soon uncomfortably wet. But the weather failed to dampen the enthusiasm of the crowd as donations of over £4,000 in loose change dropped into buckets and was collected and counted by members of Norfolk's Lions Clubs.

One particular photograph of Jill, published by the local press, inadvertently caused a series of life-changing events. When appropriate, Jill's parents, Herbert and Kate, often accompanied their daughter to functions, Herbert especially enjoying the Norwich City home matches at Carrow Road. The civic party was always royally entertained by Chairman Robert Chase, who provided a hot buffet, blankets and whisky. One morning, a photo of the family group featured on the front cover of the newspaper. A Norwich resident recognised Herbert, who unbeknownst to him had two much older brothers who had both emigrated to Canada before Herbert was born. Family estrangements meant Herbert was never told about his siblings. But someone knew, and that person sent the cutting to the son of one of his brothers, Herbert's nephew Ken, who immediately made contact with City Hall in Norwich. The family was reunited when Ken and his wife visited Norwich later that year and Jill delighted in entertaining them in the Lord Mayor's Parlour. Sadly, both Herbert's older brothers had since died, but the old man was thrilled to meet a long-lost nephew.

Jill's grand finale was the twentieth anniversary of RAF Coltishall being bestowed with the Freedom of the City of Norwich in 1967. The assembled crowd was treated to a feast of colour and pageantry, including three squadrons marching with fixed bayonets to the beat of three military bands. A formation of four Jaguar fighters flew low over the city, timed exactly to coincide with events on the ground. Jill inspected the troops and veterans outside City Hall, alongside RAF Coltishall Commanding Officer, Group Captain Mike French, and Police Superintendent Roger Brighton. The Lord Mayor had difficulty maintaining her composure, unable to believe just how far she had come.

At the end of May 1987, two weeks after Kim's wedding, Jill graciously stood down in favour of Conservative Councillor Garry Wheatley, with Len Stevenson taking over as Sheriff. The civic coach made its way through the Heigham Street traffic to collect Jill and Brian for their final ride as civic leaders, watched by curious neighbours. Jill had enjoyed every minute of her year, but most significant were the numerous opportunities to help the elderly and the homeless. Her only regret was not having been able to influence the building of more sheltered housing in the city, a constant challenge for local authorities.

Two years later, in 1989, Jill became Sheriff of Norwich, working with Lord Mayor David Fullman. This was also the year they welcomed grandson James into the family. In an unprecedented move in 1991, impressed by her approach to the role and in recognition that she would not be standing for council again in 1992, the city offered Jill the purple robe once again, this time serving with Lord Mayor Philip Moore. Both terms of civic office brought her new adventures, professionally and personally, as she travelled to meetings of the National Sheriffs' Association and also hosted her granddaughter Charlotte's christening party in the historic Guildhall.

Today, she continues as a loyal member of the Civic Association, enthusiastically attending functions when her health allows, catching up with friends and colleagues. Although no longer styling hair herself, the business continues with the loyal Glenda in charge, the salon looking much the same as it has for decades, with a full-length, slightly faded photograph of Jill as Lord Mayor hanging over a basin. Brian is never far away and the couple are much loved and held in high esteem by all who know them. Jill still recalls with pleasure a comment made to her by Patricia Hollis, since appointed a baroness in the House of Lords: 'If we could have you as Lord Mayor every year, Jill, we would.'

Endnotes

1. www.georgeplunkett.co.uk
2. The Model School for Girls educated thousands of girls from 1708 to the mid-1950s, when it merged with Bluebell School, and the name disappeared from the education scene.
3. So called because Jill was supposed to be called Gillian, but Herbert spelt her name wrongly at the Registrar's office.
4. Joyce Morgan was Lord Mayor of Norwich 1975–76.
5. Lord Mayor of Norwich 1994–95.
6. Lord Mayor of Norwich 1985–86.
7. Lord Mayor of Norwich 1979–80.
8. Baroness Hollis of Heigham was the first female Leader of Norwich City Council (1983–88), and was awarded the Freedom of the City in December 2007.
9. See chapter on Barbara Stevenson.
10. In 2017, Glenda continues to work part-time in Jill's salon.
11. Flatt, Jane, interview piece in *Eastern Daily Press*, 1 August 1986.
12. *Ibid.*
13. Scrivens, P., *Escaping Hitler: A Jewish Boy's Quest for Freedom and His Future*, Pen & Sword, Barnsley, 2016.
14. The other was Sir Arthur South, furrier by profession, Lord Mayor in 1953,

Freeman of Norwich and Chairman of Norwich City Football Club from 1973. He died in 2003, aged eighty-nine.

15. Zaharat came from a privileged background in Pakistan (Bangladesh from 1971), where she was an actress and television announcer. During the 1960s she studied at the University of Michigan in the US, where Jackie Onassis and actor Marlon Brando were amongst her friends. In 1974, she moved with her first husband, David Power, to Bracondale, Norwich, where he died a short time later.

16. The alliance was formed from the Social Democratic Party and the Liberal Party, existing from 1981 to 1988, when the two parties merged to form the Social and Liberal Democrats, later renamed the Liberal Democrats.

Jill Betty Miller 1986–87

Further Highlights from her Mayoral Year

- Welcoming the Pakistan Ambassador, Mr Ali Arshad, on his first visit to Norwich and joining the Sheriff and his wife Zaharat as they entertained him at the Guildhall.

- Having tea with the Lord Mayor of London, David Rowe-Ham, before dining that evening in Mansion House in the presence of the Prince and Princess of Wales at the launch of the Prince's Youth Business Trust.

- Lighting the city bonfire on Guy Fawkes Night, marvelling at the fireworks, fire-eaters and fire jugglers before judging the Best Guy Competition.

- Hosting a 'hen party' in the Lord Mayor's Parlour for seven other East Anglian female Lord Mayors, marking the rise of 'Petticoat Power'.

- Planting the first of fifty trees at the start of National Tree Week in Aylsham Road, Norwich.

- Greeting the Duke of Kent at a performance of *Carmen* by Kent Opera at the Theatre Royal.

- Waving off the annual convoy of lorries from East Coast Truckers, with disadvantaged children having a day out at Pleasurewood Hills in Lowestoft.

- Releasing 2,000 yellow and green balloons at Carrow Road Football Stadium alongside the Duchess of Kent when opening the new City Stand. The subsequent match against Manchester City resulted in a 1–1 draw.

- Meeting Olympic champion Sebastian Coe and footballer Trevor Brooking at the Service to Sports Awards at Pinebanks Sports and Leisure Centre.

- Enjoying the jazz band and wine at the opening of the Norwich Advice Arcade, the first of its kind in the UK, where thirty help organisations were invited to set up their offices.

- Strutting her stuff to *The Birdie Song* at a luncheon dance to celebrate the twenty-eighth anniversary of the Norwich Lions Club.

- Buying a painting from Norwich artist Tom Griffiths, husband to former Lord Mayor Jessie Griffiths, and officially presenting it as a gift to the City Council in the presence of Jessie and Tom.

CHAPTER 9

Brenda Ferris-Rampley
(1938–)
Lord Mayor of Norwich 1994–95

Norwich born and bred as I am, I've always loved my native city, although in fact as a child we usually lived just outside the city boundaries. Apart from during the war, that is, when my parents kept a sweetshop and library as well as running the Auto School of Motoring from Botolph Street. I remember cowering in the shelter as the bombs of the blitz thundered down around us. We then moved to Cromer Road near the Air Base, where the airport is now. I would skip on the pavement and the American airmen would walk past. I'd drop my rope and say, 'Got any gum, chum?'

(Brenda Ferris, speaking in 2016)

As 1994 approached, the Leader of Norwich City Council, Labour politician and history teacher Councillor Alan Waters, considered how best to celebrate the forthcoming 800th anniversary of the Norwich Charter of 1194, awarded to the city by Richard I. It was the first time that Norwich had been referred to as a city, the document conferring a new level of self-governance. A year-long, citywide Norwich 800 Festival would both entertain and educate. Alan worked on his mission statement, settling on: 'To look at the past, celebrate the present and plan for the future.'[1]

A festival would need the full backing of the Lord Mayor. Alan was confident that the nominee, Councillor Brenda Ferris – Labour member for Bowthorpe since 1979 and Sheriff of Norwich 1992 – would supply the energy, commitment and excellent networking skills necessary for this mission. For this particular year, civics and politicians would work closely together as a strong, effective team. The timing could not have been better. Very soon the results of a major local government review would be published. Norwich was hoping to regain its status as a unitary authority, winning back powers lost to Norfolk County Council in 1974. The festival would be an ideal vehicle for highlighting the cause.

Brenda was looking forward to holding office again and set about shedding a few pounds and restyling her hair. Having already set the precedent when Sheriff, Brenda again requested her married name of Ferris be linked to her maiden name of Rampley, thereby ensuring its preservation on the impressive marble slabs on the landing of City Hall. Her late father, Arthur Thomas Rampley, would have approved.

The son of Charles, a farmer from Mileham in Norfolk, Arthur lost a leg in a motorcycle accident on the Aylsham Road in the summer of 1936, just three months after his marriage to Norwich girl Nellie Maud Mary Green, whose family originated in Wells-next-the-Sea on the North Norfolk coast.[2] However, he refused to allow this to blight his life, first setting up, with his wife, the Auto School of Motoring,[3] and subsequently drawing on his farming expertise and establishing Grain Storage (Norfolk) Limited. There were three Rampley girls: Brenda April, Barbara and Veronica. Brenda was born on 6 April 1938; less than eighteen months later, Britain was at war with Germany. Because of his artificial leg, Arthur was assigned to the War Agricultural Commission, helping to run farms and occasionally working on the Royal Estate at Sandringham. Brenda and her mother spent many nights in their Anderson shelter in Botolph Street, snuggled under an eiderdown waiting for the all-clear to sound. Fearing further bombing, Arthur sent his growing family to stay with a cousin in the rural village of Wacton, 13 miles south-west of Norwich, from where Brenda can remember watching the lights and flashes from the city as the Luftwaffe rained down death and destruction.

When the hostilities were over, and his business was flourishing, Arthur rented the historic Earlham Lodge, owned by the Gurney family.[4] The girls loved living in this spacious double-fronted late seventeenth-century house, making good use of the tennis court. Arthur and Nellie sent 6-year-old Brenda to the prestigious fee-paying Norwich High School for Girls. She proved a bright child, excelling at foreign languages, with an aptitude for passing exams. Later she attended Underwood Secretarial College in Prince of Wales Road, typing to music and studying shorthand under the watchful eye of Miss Leeder, who was notorious for outlawing coloured stockings and banning boys from the premises.[5]

Brenda's diligence was rewarded with an offer to read German at University College London. A year younger than most of her fellow school leavers, she first took a gap year, teaching English for three months at a commercial private college in the city of Aachen in Germany. In 1956, on arrival at UCL, Brenda was instantly attracted to the Economics Department, switching courses to study Political Economy. It was a radical time to be a student. She joined marches and demonstrations protesting against the government's handling of the Suez Crisis, chanting 'Eden must go', while being charged by police horses in Parliament Square. She was inspired by Labour politician Aneurin Bevan speaking in Trafalgar Square, and she soon became Secretary of the Jevons Society, which was named after one of the foremost economists of the nineteenth century. She specialised in International Relations with a syllabus including International Law, International Organisations and Peace & Security. She quickly rejected her family's Conservative leanings, her emerging political awareness drawing her to the Labour Party, along with many of her likeminded university colleagues.

It was those same friends who invaded Earlham Lodge in April 1959 for Brenda's twenty-first birthday party. Four years later, when the University of East Anglia first opened, the house was integrated into the campus and the Rampley family was on the move again. Arthur was ready to invest in property and their next home, bought for £3,000, was Old Thorpe House, a former girls' school built in 1738 overlooking the river Yare. It offered spacious living areas, Georgian features, five bedrooms, cool dark cellars and half an acre of gardens. Arthur and Nellie were impressed to learn that this rambling house once belonged to Horatio Suckling, the uncle of Lord Nelson.

For Brenda the freedom and opportunities of university life proved intoxicating. She immersed herself in travel and voluntary work. Her many adventures included working in Austria at a camp for displaced persons, visiting Dubrovnik, and getting drunk for the first time in Naples! In 1958 she became involved in an internship organisation called AIESEC, working at the Hotel Viking in Oslo and another in Sweden, where she met international students including a charming

Dutchman, Alf, who was to become the Dutch Ambassador to Pakistan. Brenda applied for a job in Amsterdam with Van Leer, a supplier of steel drums to the oil industry, impressing her employer with a BSc in Economics. Every weekend she travelled to Leiden or to The Hague to spend time with Alf, learning Dutch and sharing a hitchhiking trip to Stockholm and back. However, when offered a temporary job in Brussels, working with the pool of English translators at the European Commission, it was too good an opportunity to turn down. Brussels had a lively international population, great nightlife and excellent food. The party lifestyle suited the effervescent Brenda. Norwich seemed far away and in due course, Alf became history.

Brenda left Brussels in 1963 to share a London flat in Notting Hill with her sister Barbara. When a vacancy arose at the world-renowned revolutionary Theatre Workshop in Stratford East, Brenda became a personal assistant to Joan Littlewood and her partner Gerry Raffles. Joan was described as 'the most galvanising director in mid-twentieth-century Britain'.[6] Brenda recalls working with many now famous names, including a young Barbara Windsor, Roy Kinnear and Brian Murphy. Theatre Workshop's best-known production, *Oh What a Lovely War*, had already transferred to the West End by the time Brenda arrived but there was still plenty of work to do with touring companies in the UK and New York.

One of the many after-show parties in Earls Court was to prove life-changing. Here Brenda met the charismatic Mike Ferris, a Jaguar-trained engineer and tyre salesman for Pirelli in Essex. Before long, the two were dating, impetuously agreeing after only a few months to marry, which they did on 18 December 1965. Brenda's father offered Mike a job in Norwich as an engineer with Grain Storage. After the wedding, Brenda's life took a domestic turn, living in Grove Avenue and giving birth to daughter Caitlin in 1967 and son Sean in 1969. For some years a stay-at-home mum, she helped set up a playgroup. In need of mental stimulation, she sourced translation work and when the time was right, set up her own company, Babel Translations. This venture was successful for many decades, with Brenda translating Dutch, German and French documents into English.

Once back in Norwich, Brenda rediscovered the Bystanders Society, of which she was a founder member, and introduced her husband to her old friends. Mike soon became known as 'Mr Charisma', playing cricket and football, and eventually becoming president of this independent city social club. The couple shared a passion for local politics, and in

1973 Mike was elected to represent the small market town of Loddon on Norfolk County Council. Brenda and Mike later worked together in his unsuccessful bid to become Labour MP for the Isle of Ely.

In 1977, during a family holiday in Spain, word reached them that Brenda's father had suffered a stroke. They arrived home too late to say goodbye. Arthur died on 16 June at only sixty-seven. A few months later, Brenda's grandmother died. It had been a difficult year. With the children growing more independent, Brenda became the administrator of the Norfolk and Norwich Film Theatre (NNFT), arranging monthly film showings at the Noverre Cinema in the Assembly House, as well as at the university and the Central Library. NNFT was actively seeking a permanent home when Bob Brister, Leisure Officer at City Hall, mentioned that the Stuart and Suckling Halls, donated in 1925 to the city by Ethel and Helen Colman, might be available. The vision became a reality when the building was converted to a 230-seater independent cinema, opening in April 1978 as Cinema City. Initially the NNFT volunteers ran the operation, taking turns to staff the bar and act as ushers, while 'Auntie Brenda' introduced the children's matinees.

In recognition of her role with Cinema City, the British Film Institute invited Brenda to serve as a governor. She travelled to London for meetings every month or so, becoming involved in the drafting of a national arts and media strategy, working with Richard Attenborough and Joan Bakewell. In September 1995, she met Hollywood legend Clint Eastwood at the opening of his mature couple romance movie *Bridges of Madison County*. She whispered to him how much his film represented her dream scenario, positively glowing as, with a twinkle, he responded, 'Mine too'.[7]

Early in 1979, Brenda won a City Council seat in Earlham Ward, soon thereafter renamed as Bowthorpe, and colleagues were impressed by her commitment. However, within a short while Brenda was shocked to be diagnosed with breast cancer and underwent a mastectomy. Around the same time, Mike's charms proved irresistible to another and in 1981, while emerging from chemotherapy, Brenda found herself in the throes of a divorce and facing life as a single parent. Brenda and her two children, Caitlin and Sean, moved into a new home in 1983. She fell in love with an 1851 double-fronted terrace house with garden front and back, painted portico and generous windows in a quiet location just off Dereham Road. Very soon the walls were filled with art works of all styles, shelves laden with books and favourite pieces of Victoriana, and her desk awash with correspondence, agendas and reports. As her strength returned, Brenda looked forward to getting back to work. She had lost none of her passion, and once again became fully involved as a frank and forthright committee member, an effective chair and, for many, a formidable opponent.

By 1992, Brenda was nominated as Sheriff of Norwich, serving with Lord Mayor Arthur Clare. The Lady Mayoress was Zaharat Power-Clare, Arthur's second wife.[8] Brenda and Zaharat could not have been more different. For the most part the two ladies tolerated each other with dignity, but in February 1993 there were angry exchanges over the unauthorised display by Zaharat of artificial roses in a public area of City Hall. Both local and national newspapers carried the story, which was billed as 'The War of the Roses'. Brenda proved to be an excellent Sheriff and ambassador for the city, so much so that two years later, the Labour group nominated her as Lord Mayor for 1994–95. She chose Norwich Breast Cancer Research Fund to be her charity, explaining that having 'come through the terrifying ordeal thirteen years earlier, I now want to help other women facing the nightmare of breast cancer.'[9] As a single woman, Brenda chose not to have an official consort, instead picking out specific friends, family members or colleagues and matching them to events she knew would reflect their interests. A former senior lecturer at Norwich City College, Bill Carpenter would be her Sheriff. The civic team was complete.

The brochure for the Norwich 800 celebrations promised hot air balloons, a mammoth community fête including the biggest teddy bears' picnic in the world, the Discovery 800 Exhibition charting the history of the city, medieval banquets, street parties and a plethora of souvenir merchandise including mugs, mustard pots, a brass commemorative medal, a special traditional ale brewed by the Reindeer Brewery, and even bespoke Norwich 800 BT phone cards.

But on Monday, 1 August, the events of the summer were rudely interrupted when cleaners arrived for work at the Central Library and Archives. Darren Fox was alerted by an alarm, set off when a strip light in the American room had blown. Darren was horrified to find flames coming from behind a bookcase. Within thirty minutes the building was an inferno. Fire crews from all over the county used turntable ladders and high-powered water jets in a concerted effort to douse the flames. At 8.00 pm, Anglian Water increased the pressure on the mains to allow more water to flow. A thick pall of smoke hung over the city as priceless documents tracing the history of Norwich were reduced to ashes. At 10.00 am, bystanders watched stunned as firefighters

Ethel (right) and Helen Colman
in the garden of Carrow Abbey.

Ethel Mary Colman,
Lord Mayor of
Norwich 1923–24.

The original *Hathor* on the Nile, where Alan Colman died in 1897.

Mabel Clarkson at her
home in Mount Pleasant,
Norwich, 1928.

Mabel Clarkson, Lord
Mayor of Norwich
1930–31, presenting
prizes at a carnival in aid
of Norfolk and Norwich
Hospital, 9 July 1931.

Ruth Hardy, Lord Mayor of Norwich 1950–51, with Marion, her daughter and Lady Mayoress.

Ruth presents a Norfolk farmer with a rosette for his livestock at the Royal Norfolk Show, held at Anmer Park, Sandringham, 28–29 June 1950.

Jessie Griffiths, Lord Mayor of Norwich 1969–70.

Jessie and Tom Griffiths presented with sprigs of shamrock at a St Patrick's Night dinner, 17 March 1970.

Joyce Morgan, Lord Mayor of Norwich 1975–76, Margaret Thatcher, Leader of the Conservative Party, and Jessie Griffiths in the Lord Mayor's Parlour, 14 November 1975.

Joyce Morgan, Selina Morgan and Gwilym Morgan travelling to City Hall in the civic coach, 19 May 1976.

Valerie Guttsman, Lord Mayor of Norwich 1979–80 on Mayor-Making Day, 15 May 1979, with the Guildhall in the distance.

Valerie Guttsman performing a topping out ceremony at Norwich Job Centre, Theatre Street, 13 June 1979.

Barbara Stevenson, Lord Mayor of Norwich 1985–86, in the Lord Mayor's Procession, 15 July 1985.

Four generations at Barbara Stevenson's Mayor-Making: Len Stevenson, Jonathan, Barbara, Alice Yallop, Anya and Gavin.

Barbara Stevenson (née Yallop, left), with two of her sisters, Olive and Ivy, at their farm in Bedlingham, Norfolk, in the late 1920s.

Jill Miller, Lord Mayor of Norwich 1986–87.

Jill Miller with Zaharat Power-Clare.

Jill Miller cutting husband Brian's hair in 1986.

Brenda Ferris with actor Clint Eastwood at the British Film Institute, 1995.

Portrait of Brenda Ferris, Lord Mayor of Norwich 1994–95, by Dave Chedgey.

Lord Mayor Brenda Ferris celebrating Norwich 800 Festival in 1994.

Lila appearing as Dolly Levin in *The Matchmaker*, Great Hall Players, 1986.

Lila Cooper, Lord Mayor of Norwich 1995–96.

The civic coach driving through Norvic Drive to collect Lila, June 1995.

Robert Climie, MP for
Kilmarnock, 1923–24 and 1929.

Joyce Climie Divers, Lord Mayor of
Norwich 2004–2005, on the balcony of the
Lord Mayor's Parlour.

Cloth bag
designed by
Jeremy Deller,
Norwich
University of
the Arts.

Felicity Hartley, Lord Mayor of Norwich
2006–2007, with her son Christopher.

Christopher, Felicity and Sheriff of Norwich John Drake.

Eve Collishaw with her dog Rufus and artist Liz Balkwill.

Eve Collishaw, Lord Mayor of Norwich 2009–10, with Sheriff Tim O'Riordan, holding the League One Champions' trophy for 2009–10, won by Norwich City Football Club.

Ken and Jenny on their engagement in 1958.

Ken Lay, Jenny Lay, Lord Mayor of Norwich 2011–12, Chris Higgins, Sheriff of Norwich, and Glynis Higgins.

Judith Lubbock, Lord Mayor of Norwich 2014–15, canoeing with John Packman, CEO of Broads Authority, November 2014.

Judith Lubbock inspects troops at the Battle of Britain Parade, 15 September 2014.

Left to right: Dean of Norwich Cathedral Jane Hedges, Sheriff Beryl Blower, Lord Mayor of Norwich 2015–16 Brenda Arthur, and Archdeacon of Norwich Jan McFarlane, pictured before the Civic Service on 21 June 2015.

Brenda Arthur and her grandchildren, Niamh, Evan, Dylan and twins Grayson and Adrienne, photographed on the balcony outside the Lord Mayor's Parlour.

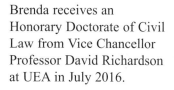

Brenda receives an Honorary Doctorate of Civil Law from Vice Chancellor Professor David Richardson at UEA in July 2016.

Sheriff Richard Marks and Lord Mayor of Norwich 2016–17 Marion Maxwell on City Hall steps following their Mayor-Making, 24 May 2016.

Marion welcomes Her Majesty the Queen to the Fiji: Art & Life exhibition at the Sainsbury Centre for Visual Arts at UEA, 27 January 2017.

Norwich City Council sword and mace bearers Robert Sabberton, Gavin Thorpe and Wayne Hum, 2015.

Whifflers with Snap the Dragon, Civic Service 2015.

The Council Chamber in Norwich City Hall, Mayor-Making Day 2014.

The civic coach, driven by John Parker, outside Norwich Cathedral for the Annual Justice Service, October 2011.

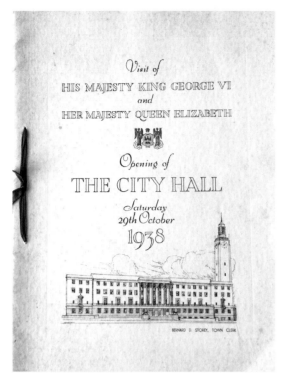

Souvenir brochure for Norwich Festival, June 1951, with cover design by Tom Griffiths.

Souvenir brochure for the Opening of the City Hall, 1938.

Past Lord Mayor badge.

Motif on chain celebrating Norwich's status as a UNESCO City of Literature.

Angels motif reflecting the angels found on and in City Hall, denoting the title of Lord Mayor.

Chocolate motif from the new Lord Mayor's chain, 2016, celebrating Norwich's relationship with chocolate.

brought out shopping trolleys filled with damaged documents and blistered books. Alerted by council staff, Brenda arrived on the scene, looking on from City Hall roof as the drama unfolded. By 1.00 pm, with the library still alight, staff were offered a crumb of comfort when they learnt that many priceless documents had been saved by virtue of being stored underground behind steel doors.[10] Tragically, the unique Second Division USAAF Memorial Room, built up as a lasting memorial to the heroism of US airmen, had taken the worst of the blaze, losing 3,500 books and archive material. The library, opened in 1963 by the Queen Mother, had undergone a major refit only three months earlier. The following morning the local press published photographs of the devastated Lord Mayor, openly crying alongside tearful library staff.

Spring 1995 brought a much-anticipated visit to the French medieval city of Rouen, twinned with Norwich since 1959. Brenda enjoyed using her language skills as she represented Norwich at sumptuous dinners and official visits. She arrived home on 11 April feeling a new sense of optimism. It was not to last. The following morning, a further disaster befell one of the city's most iconic venues. The Assembly House, a Grade I listed building and the epitome of Georgian elegance, had been opened as a public space in 1755 and quickly became the centre of Norwich society. Two hundred and forty years later, much to the dismay of the city, fire destroyed the magnificent Music Room, restaurant area and Grand Hall. Fortunately, many paintings and items of furniture were recovered and much of the wooden panelling and Georgian plasterwork remained intact.[11] Once again, Brenda was devastated, but still managed to fulfil her engagement that evening at the Norwich City versus Nottingham Forest match. If the Canaries lost this one, then relegation to the First Division was almost inevitable.[12] Nottingham won 0–1. It had not been a good day.

With Norwich 800 nearing its finale, Brenda performed an unusual task at the foot of City Hall steps on 13 May. Watched by traditionally dressed mace bearers and attendants, with the Sheriff at her side, Brenda balanced precariously over a deep hole in the pavement, gripping tightly to the straps around a large metal box as it was lowered deeper and deeper. The Norwich 800 Time Capsule held instructions that it was not to be reopened until the year 2095. The contents included photographs of Norwich children born on 5 May 1994 (in the hope that at least one might still be alive in 2095), Royal Mail first day covers, a signed football from Norwich City Football Club, a copy of the Highway Code, lottery tickets and, bizarrely, a pair of Lycra leggings – intended as a symbol of freedom for women in the 1990s.

On Tuesday, 16 May 1995, Brenda's twelve months in office were at an end. She remained a councillor for Bowthorpe until 2008, when she lost the seat to the Conservative candidate. For a number of years Brenda was privileged to serve as one of Norfolk's Deputy Lieutenants. She is a trustee of Norwich Consolidated Charities, Chair of the Norfolk Contemporary Art Society and Chair of Mancroft Ward Labour Party. She is proud to be grandmother to Josh and Louis, the children of daughter Caitlin, a successful barrister. Her son Sean works in Devon as a renowned homeopathic dowser, specialising in the diagnosis and treatment of long-term illnesses. Now in her late seventies, Brenda shows few signs of slowing down.

There is a postscript to the Time Capsule story: sometime later, an opportunist thief stole the engraved metal lid marking the spot, probably to sell as scrap. With the minimum of publicity, the Council hurriedly replaced it with a cement cover, carrying the identical inscription, which remains in place to this day. Brenda can be confident that, barring a catastrophic road-widening scheme, the Norwich public will walk across her name until the end of the twenty-first century.

Endnotes

1. Councillor Alan Waters, speaking in 2016.
2. Nellie's ancestor William Green lost his life during the Wells' Lifeboat disaster of October 1880, when eleven members of the crew drowned attempting to save the ship *Ocean Queen*.
3. The Auto School of Motoring did not close for business until 1991, a testimony to the energy and business acumen of Brenda's mother Nellie.
4. A Norfolk family of Quakers who over many centuries had a major influence on Norwich. The family bank merged into Barclays in 1896.
5. *East Anglian Daily Times*, 'Writing on all four sides of the paper', author unknown, 5 March 2012.
6. As described by pioneering theatre director Peter Brook, whom Joan allegedly despised.
7. Brenda Ferris, talking in 2016.
8. See chapter on Jill Miller.
9. *Evening News*, 17 May 1994.
10. These included the ancient seal given to the city by Richard the Lionheart, parish registers dating from AD 650 and original handwritten manuscripts of Sir Henry Rider Haggard novels *She* and *King Solomon's Mines*.

11. After eighteen months of fundraising the building was restored to its former glory and reopened on Valentine's Day 1997.
12. The 1994–95 season finished badly with Norwich City third from bottom of the Premier League table and relegated to Division One. The club was saved from bankruptcy over the next few days by the efforts of Geoffrey Watling, Delia Smith and Michael Wynn-Jones. The team had to wait until 2004 for a return to the Premier League.

Brenda Ferris-Rampley 1994–95

Further Highlights from her Mayoral Year

- Hosting a civic reception at Blackfriars Hall to launch Norwich 800 and witnessing the hanging of a commissioned painting for Norwich 800 by artist Louise Richardson. Eating a slice of the sugar-crafted Norwich 800 cake, washed down with Norwich 800 Traditional Ale.

- Holding a book signing at City Hall for schoolfriend novelist Judith Saxton (aka Katie Flynn), celebrating the publication of her fiftieth novel, *Someone Special*.

- Overcoming a fear of heights when climbing aboard a hot air balloon and taking to the skies momentarily, at the Norwich 800 Hot Air Balloon Fiesta in Earlham Park.

- Greeting Her Majesty the Queen and His Royal Highness the Duke of Edinburgh at the University of East Anglia when they opened the new Occupational Health and Physiotherapy building, to be known as The Queen's Building.

- Indulging a love of birdwatching when opening Whitlingham Marsh Nature Reserve in Thorpe St Andrew. Enjoying watching out for grey herons, gadwalls and kingfishers from the privacy of a hide – the first of its kind in the city.

- Welcoming eighty newborn babies to City Hall, each born on Norwich 800 Launch Day, and presenting their parents with commemorative envelopes donated by the Royal Mail and stamped with the babies' special birth date, 17 May 1994.

- Being the first Lord Mayor to walk in front of the Lord Mayors' Procession as schools and groups depicted scenes from the history of Norwich. Announcing that £4,507 had been raised for local charities.

- Holding a civic reception in the Advice Arcade Gallery to mark the opening of an art exhibition called On the Wall – A Sister Show. Admiring the collection of co-operative work, each reflecting the lives of women.

- Sailing from Norwich to Thorpe River Green in a historic pleasure wherry as part of the 'Wherries on the Wensum' spectacular, complete with a dragon boat, vintage wooden vessels and steam drifter *Lydia Eva*.

- Hosting a Chinese takeaway lunch in the Parlour with the actor Victor Spinetti (performing in *Aladdin* at the Theatre Royal), an old friend from her Theatre Workshop days.

- Taking the salute from servicemen, including the men and women of the 2nd Air Division 8th USAAF, on 7 May 1995, the fiftieth anniversary of Victory in Europe Day.

CHAPTER 10

Lila Divi Cooper
(1931–2000)

Lord Mayor of Norwich 1995–96

During the early nineties, Lila was one of only two Conservative councillors on the City Council. She was supportive of us becoming a Unitary Authority. She was slim and elegant and apparently half-Indian. We were all very white middle class in the Council Chamber. We were having this discussion that we needed more councillors from ethnic minorities and Lila said, 'I can do it.' I think she told me she had a sister who looked partly Indian heritage, with dark hair, but Lila had pale skin and blonde hair, so we were surprised.

(Alan Waters, Labour Leader Norwich City Council, speaking in 2016)

On the evening of 6 March 1990, a budget meeting was taking place in City Hall, Norwich. As councillors perused their agenda papers, a large crowd of protestors gathered in St Peter's Street, waving placards and shouting abusive slogans. As hundreds fought their way past police, jostling for a place in the public gallery, a breakaway group broke into the basement, locking the doors behind them, their mission to smash up computers and destroy council documents. Outside, others trampled over cars parked in the rear car park. The meeting upstairs was abandoned when protestors draped sheets daubed with slogans over the public gallery, throwing heavy council agendas onto the floor below, showering the Labour benches. Lord Mayor David Fullman was heckled, the mob chanting their disgust at the planned introduction of the so-called poll tax, an unpopular community tax, first introduced into Scotland by Margaret Thatcher's Conservative government a year previously and now about to be implemented throughout the UK.[1]

At that time only three Conservatives held seats on Norwich City Council. With Garry Wheatley absent that evening, the remaining two, Judith Virgo and Lila Cooper, felt exposed. Judith remembers the occasion vividly:

> We started proceedings and it was total uproar. The officers were in a horseshoe in the middle. We couldn't help thinking that the agendas were hitting people who didn't agree with the policy either! The police forcibly cleared the public gallery before locking us in the Council Chamber.[2]

At about 8.30 pm, the bulk of the crowd now dispersed, the police escorted the shaken councillors and staff from the premises. Lila called her husband. Gary arrived quickly and drove them home, where he poured both ladies a stiff gin and tonic.

Lila Divi was born in Surrey on 16 January 1931, her names originating from the Indian sub-continent, giving credence to the suggestion that Lila was a mixed-race baby. She was educated at Camden School for Girls in London, before serving five years in the WRNS, achieving the rank of petty officer wren. Her husband Ernest served in RAF Bomber Command, where comrades dubbed him Gary, after the veteran Hollywood actor Gary Cooper, a name he was known as for the rest of his life. In 1955, their son Peter was born, prompting Lila and Gary to leave the services and emigrate to Ontario in Canada in 1957. Lila worked for a finance company before the family returned to the UK after five years, settling in Gary's home city of Norwich. In 1963, with Peter now at school, Lila took a job at Peat Marwick McLintock (KPMG), a firm of Norwich accountants. She remained a loyal employee for twenty-eight years, retiring as a supervisor in 1991, aged sixty. But it was her passion for local politics and amateur dramatics that defined her for nearly four decades.

The Great Hall Theatre Company began as a private theatre club in 1961, founded by Donald Pyle. In 1964, a small acting space was created at the Bakers Arms in Heigham Street, where the first general meeting of Great Hall Players took place on Sunday, 27 November 1966. It was noted that 'Mr Keith Law would be glad of some help with serving sherry during performances.' There is no evidence that Lila was a member from the outset, but she is listed as treasurer at a meeting held in June 1974. It was during this year that the group moved premises to the Friends Meeting House in Upper Goat Lane, a venue that endured until 1986. It was not ideal, with the Players dealing with performance in the round, a high ceiling with difficult acoustics, religious sensitivity over the sale of alcohol, challenges with lighting, limited storage and cramped dressing rooms. But with the group's popularity increasing, greater audience capacity offset any inconveniences.

In November 1974, Lila played Miss Cooper, a hotel manageress, in *Separate Tables* by Terence Rattigan, the first production at the new venue. Neville Miller, critiquing the play in the *Eastern Evening News*, commented, 'Lila Cooper was impressive. In everything that requires sympathy she comes over strongly.' In the autumn of 1975, Lila took on the task of directing a production of *Arsenic and Old Lace* by Joseph Kesselring, working with fourteen actors. Over the next seventeen years, Lila would appear in more than twenty productions, her poise, elegance, modulated tones and natural affinity with comedy attracting excellent reviews. She also directed eleven plays, including classics such as *Lion in Winter*, *The Odd Couple* and *Rebecca*, as well as working full time, bringing up her son and carrying out her duties as a city councillor.

Long before the 1976 local elections, when Lila first won a council seat for St Stephen's Ward, she served on the executive council of Norwich Conservative Association, worked with Bignold Junior and Middle Schools, and sat on the committee of her local residents' association. Lila remained a Conservative councillor for nearly twenty years, enjoying her role in opposition, battling against a consistently Labour controlled council. As an experienced actress, expounding her views held no fear, and Lila proved to be an outspoken yet eloquent opponent in the Council Chamber. Eight years later, in 1984, Lila was invited to become Sheriff of Norwich, working alongside Lord Mayor Stanley Petersen. Since the early 1980s, Lila had been Chairman of Great Hall Players. Her final part before becoming Sheriff was as an unsympathetic prison officer in *The Enquiry*, by Charlotte Hastings. Her name would not appear on a theatre programme for a further two years. She had a more important role to play.

As Sheriff, as in her everyday life, Lila was always immaculately turned out with matching shoes, gloves and handbag, her hair never out of place, and her deportment and style much admired by female colleagues. The art of looking good is often dependent on good foundations. Former Lady Mayoress Pam Petersen recalls attending a Royal Garden Party at Buckingham Palace with Lila. 'On the drive down she insisted on stopping at her mother's flat in Surrey to get changed. I will never forget the vision of Lila in a full corset!'

One occasion Lila preferred to forget was when thieves broke into the official Daimler, left unattended while Lord Mayor Stanley Petersen was attending an old people's luncheon club near St John's RC Cathedral. Unfortunately, the eighteenth-century 22-carat Sheriff's chain, valued at £5,000, was locked inside, ready for when Lila joined the Lord Mayor later that afternoon. Distraught, Lila made a public appeal, offering to travel anywhere to retrieve it. Council Leader Patricia Hollis was horrified, describing the missing chain as an important part of the finest collection of civic regalia in any city outside London, likening the crime to 'pillage and loot'.[3] The chain was never found, and the press reminded Lila of this embarrassing incident for many years to come.[4]

Early in 1985, Lila, now a doting grandmother to baby Elizabeth Sarah, received an official invitation from the new Sheriff of Gloucester, City Councillor Andrew Gavells, inviting her to his city, along with the fourteen other civic Sheriffs in England and Wales, suggesting that they 'meet together to discuss our roles and problems, and even try to ensure that the office does not disappear altogether, as there are now only a few of us left.'[5] Lila joined the meeting, helping to establish the National Association of City and Town Sheriffs of England and Wales (NACTSEW). Membership was opened to all past and serving Sheriffs, with Lila appointed as only the second Chairman of the Association. On the occasion of her re-election as Chairman in 1989, Lila failed to reach the venue in Southampton after she and Gary were involved in a road accident. Lila broke three ribs and spent the night in hospital before returning to Norwich, her re-election taking place in her absence. A number of Sheriffs of Norwich have been, and continue to be, involved in the Association; past attendees include Jenny Lay, Doug Underwood, Jill Miller, Ralph Gayton and William Armstrong.

Having completed her year as Sheriff, Lila was free to rejoin her beloved Great Hall Players, relax in the company of friends and return to her former bad habits of swearing and smoking when under pressure! Late in 1986, she was cast as Dolly Levi, the central character of *The Matchmaker*, a comedy by Thornton Wilder, which had been re-imagined in 1969 by the Hollywood musical success *Hello Dolly*. A local reviewer commented, 'Lila gives a quietly sincere interpretation of the scheming mind behind an outwardly charming appearance.'[6]

From the early 1990s, it was Lila's mind that began to preoccupy members of her family, friends and colleagues. In 1989, college lecturer Judith Virgo was elected as Conservative Councillor for Eaton Ward, joining Lila in the opposition seats of Norwich City Council. The two women became close friends, the younger and less experienced Judith gleaning tips about dealing with casework and how to handle officers and Labour councillors. She noted how well Lila spoke at meetings, invariably without notes, demonstrating a quick wit and a level of self-confidence. Judith began supporting Lila's theatre productions, was added to Gary and Lila's dinner party list, and was impressed by Lila's skill at knitting stunning sweaters. Judith became a frequent guest at Lila's immaculate dinner parties. But something was not quite right. 'She told me several times that she had to get back to the doctor,' said Judith. 'She simply wasn't feeling well but couldn't put her finger on it.'

Lila made no secret of her ambition to be Lord Mayor. Late in 1994 the decision was made to offer her the role for the following year. Lila was delighted. However, during the subsequent months she began to have memory lapses, becoming a little vague and disorientated. Judith remembers one particular occasion in the Council Chamber:

> All the two of us had to do was to agree with the motion. When this item came up, I was at the back where the jugs are, pouring a glass of water. Lila got up to respond on behalf of the Conservative group but then forgot what she was supposed to say. But it was more than that. I banged the water down and sprinted down the steps, grabbing the microphone and saying, 'We would like to totally agree.' I used to go round to her house on a Sunday night and we would go through the agenda together for the following day. But gradually I realised that I would need to prepare something myself for every topic as I knew she would forget.

A confidential meeting was arranged between senior figures from the local Conservative Party and the leading group at City Hall to discuss how to handle the situation. Lila had accepted the nomination; no one wanted to withdraw it now. It was agreed that with co-operation, discretion and careful handling, it should be possible for Lila to complete her year as Lord Mayor. Councillors and staff were briefed on a 'need to know' basis, civic staff charged with helping to write Lila's speeches and ensure she wrote everything down, particularly the details of her official engagements. For the first few months everything went smoothly. Lila's Sheriff, Douglas Underwood, prepared to stand in at a moment's notice, with former Lord Mayor Brenda Ferris offering support and advice, and the drivers briefed to be vigilant. On one occasion Lila got into the car still with her hair rollers in, the driver having no choice but to mention it.

In October, Lila invited a group of thirteen former Lord Mayors, including Joyce Morgan, Valerie Guttsman and Brenda Ferris, to pose for press photographs to promote the scrapping of the current two-tier system of city and county councils serving Norwich. The verdict from the government was due by Christmas. Although as Lord Mayor Lila was supposed to remain apolitical, when declaring her aims for the year following Mayor-Making, she said, 'My main aims are to increase government funding for the people of Norwich and to have Norwich granted unitary status'[7] – a view controversially contrary to those of her colleagues in the Conservative group.

Long before Lila became Lord Mayor, plans were under way to prepare a programme of events to celebrate the 900 years since Bishop Herbert began building his new cathedral in Norwich. Suggestions included a Royal visit. At City Hall, the Civic and Member Support Officer, Heather Ashmore, felt privileged to be involved in the organisation:

> I remember going to a meeting when it was announced and the question was raised that, as the Queen was going to undertake more engagements in the afternoon, where should she have lunch? The Lord Lieutenant, Sir Timothy Colman, looked at me and said, 'Is City Hall a possibility?' and I said yes, thinking how amazing that would be.[8]

Her Majesty the Queen arrived at Norwich Cathedral on Thursday, 4 April 1996 to distribute the Royal Maundy money to 140 Norfolk men and woman, all aged over sixty-five and of modest means – unsung heroes who had given service in local Christian communities.[9] An army of volunteers had spent days brushing flagstones, polishing pews and buffing brass candlesticks. Security around Cathedral Close was tight, everyone needing an official pass to enter. As First Citizen, Lila would perform a central role during the entire day, with everyone concerned about how the stress might affect her. Heather was assigned to accompany Lila and to gently observe her every move. At exactly 10.50 am, the five cars carrying the Royal party and accompanying security staff swept through Erpingham Gate, to be greeted by the

Lord Lieutenant. With introductions and handshakes completed, the official party filed into the cathedral to take their reserved seats. The civic attendants, dressed in their ceremonial uniforms, watched aghast as the Lord Mayor went in the wrong direction and had to be rescued and escorted to her place.

City Hall also underwent a transformation in readiness for the Royal luncheon. Several florists spent the previous day filling the building with magnificent arrangements and the Mancroft Committee Room, parallel to the balcony, was opened up to create one large space, the floor vacuumed to perfection. The tables were arranged into one long top table to accommodate the Royal visitors and the civic party, and a further five tables for the rest. The mace stand was erected in between the two main windows, displaying the priceless civic regalia. Market Square was packed with exuberant onlookers when, at exactly 12.50 pm, the Royal cars arrived at Guildhall Hill and the Queen and the Duke of Edinburgh were escorted to the Lord Mayor's Parlour before joining the sixty lunch guests. The Queen was seated with the Lord Lieutenant on her left and the official host, the Lord Mayor of Norwich, on her right. The Queen had been briefed about Lila's unpredictable idiosyncrasies. As the rousing toast 'The Queen' was declared, Heather and her colleagues listened proudly from outside the wooden doors, relieved that this extremely special day had been such a success.

With Labour Councillor Rory Quinn now invested as Lord Mayor, Lila stood down as a councillor with immediate effect. At the same election, Judith Virgo lost her Eaton seat to Liberal Democrat Judith Lubbock. The City Council was now bereft of Conservative representation. For two years Lila lived quietly, her condition deteriorating and Gary taking care of her and the house as best he could. Heartbroken and exhausted, Gary died in May 1998, aged seventy-five. Lila never came to terms with his death. Following Gary's funeral, Judith rang Lila to ask how she was coping. Lila appeared unaware that her husband had gone. For weeks afterwards, Lila regularly visited City Hall, asking if anyone had seen him.

Unable to manage, Lila was admitted to the Julian Hospital, undergoing dementia assessment and later transferred to Two Acres Nursing Home in Taverham, where she died, aged sixty-nine, in November 2000. Her son Peter was stunned by the enormous number of phone calls and cards he received following the news of her death. Commenting to the *Evening News*, he said:

She was always in the minority but that never stopped her. In that type of situation she might have felt she was banging her head against a brick wall but she never lost her temper. She'd often be out in the evening sitting with an old lady from a tower block who was having problems with noise. She would always help people who came to her with problems.[10]

Endnotes

1. The policy meant that every adult in the UK would pay a community charge (based on the notional rental value of a house), regardless of income. The British public thought this to be an unfair reversal of decades of progressive taxation. At a huge protest rally in Trafalgar Square on 31 March, 100 people were hurt and 400 injured.
2. Judith Virgo, speaking in 2016.
3. *Eastern Daily Press*, 15 December 1984.
4. In 1739, wealthy merchant Thomas Emmerson gave two identical gold chains, at a cost of 100 guineas each, to the Sheriffs of Norwich. This meant that following the theft of Lila's chain in 1984, there was already another for use by subsequent Sheriffs.
5. http://www.nactsew.org.uk/history/welcome-2/
6. Ken Hulme, writing in the *Evening News*, 1986.
7. *Evening News*, 17 May 1995. The government declared that Norfolk would remain with the status quo and, despite a review, the bid for Unitary Status from Norwich City Council was turned down.
8. Heather Ashmore, speaking in 2016.
9. Tradition states that one man and one woman are chosen for each year the Queen has lived, receiving Maundy money equivalent in pence to that number of years. The Queen was seventy in 1996.
10. *Evening News*, 24 November 2000.

Lila Divi Cooper 2005–2006

Further Highlights from her Mayoral Year

- Inspecting the troops as a former Wren at Remembrance Sunday and Battle of Britain parades and nominating the Soldiers, Sailors & Air Force Association as her official Lord Mayor's Charity.

- Attending the Queen's Garden Party at Buckingham Palace with Sheriff Doug Underwood and his wife Sandra. The driver almost driving the wrong way around the roundabout at the end of the Mall and Prince Charles asking them if they had yet had a cup of tea.

- Playing bowls in Eaton Park at the Annual Howard Dakin Bowls Match, held in memory of the prosperous city merchant and Lord Mayor of Norwich 1889.

- Enjoying the Chinese dragon dancing outside City Hall when celebrating the Year of the Rat at Chinese New Year.

- Speaking at a meeting of the Norwich branch of Soroptimist International, a global association for business and professional women working to improve the lives of women and girls.

- Presenting the prizes in the Lord Mayor's Parlour to the winning floats and walking groups from the Lord Mayor's Procession.

- Riding in the civic coach with the Sheriff and Lord Lieutenant as it ferried the visiting High Court Judge to the annual Justice Service at Norwich Cathedral, to celebrate Norfolk's ancient offices of state and the county's tradition of self-administration of local justice.

- Sharing Gary's memories of his years serving with Bomber Command based at RAF Coltishall, during an official visit to the station.

- Being invited by Portsmouth City Council to attend a Freedom of the City ceremony for Lord Judd of Portsea, a former Labour Party MP and Minister for Overseas Development 1976–77. Accompanied by Heather Ashmore and other council staff, Lila met with Lord Mayors from around the UK. The party were taken on a guided tour of HMS *Victory*, Nelson's flagship at the Battle of Trafalgar in 1805.

- Walking on the new carpet in the Lord Mayor's Parlour as donated and fitted by Jarrold Department Store in time for the visit of Her Majesty the Queen and the Duke of Edinburgh on 4 April 1996.

CHAPTER 11

Joyce Anthea Climie Divers (1949–)
Lord Mayor of Norwich 2004–2005

I saw the Beatles live at The Odeon theatre in Glasgow on 3 December 1965. I was about seventeen. We couldn't hear a word of the songs. We'd queued up for tickets and there was a big riot when we came out. Mounted police herded us about. Big horses. You don't argue with them. I remember being in a French class and the teacher turned on the TV to show us something when the Beatles came on. The whole class just screamed!

(Joyce Pitty, speaking in 2016)

Shift changes at the Fairfield Shipyard on Glasgow's river Clyde were heralded by the screech of whistles and horns, followed by a tsunami of cloth caps as riveters, caulkers, blacksmiths and welders came and went. Young Joyce Climie never tired of this spectacle, visible from the family two-bedroomed council flat overlooking Elder Park, where her grandfather, Charles Climie, originally from Kilmarnock, worked as a blacksmith. His son George was a qualified chartered accountant, but during the Second World War served as a staff sergeant with responsibilities for radio communications. He met Hilda Edna Bailey, a native of Birmingham and volunteer in the Auxiliary Territorial Service (ATS). The couple married, and after the war George and his wife returned to Goven, moving in with his widowed father. Four years later, on 13 May 1949, the couple welcomed baby Joyce Anthea to their family.

With the arrival of sons Brian and David during the following six years, the tiny flat became intolerably overcrowded. George applied for an exchange to a larger council house in the more select area of Moss Park, with a view over Bellahouston Park. At school, Joyce proved a popular student; she was always top of the class and had a talent for running. Her ambitious father, aware of his daughter's potential, was delighted when the school suggested Joyce sit the entrance exam for the prestigious Hutchesons' Grammar School, founded in 1641 and known to locals as 'Hutchie'. Her father constantly pushed Joyce and her brothers to work hard and succeed. His own career was derailed through the onset of war, a time he never spoke of, and his father had never advanced beyond manual work. George Climie wanted better for his children.

In the past, a number of the extended Climie clan had become high achievers. Robert Climie, the uncle of Joyce's grandfather, was the son of a colliery fireman and a bonnet knitter. He became a trade unionist and local councillor, and in 1923 was elected as Labour MP for Kilmarnock. In 1924, he lost his seat to a Tory, only to regain it in May 1929 with a handsome majority, benefitting from women over twenty-one then having the vote. His sister was involved in establishing the Co-operative movement in Scotland and their brother, James Climie, travelled to the Klondike in America in search of gold, later becoming President of the Alaska Railroad Workers Union. Growing up, Joyce had no knowledge of these political ancestors.[1]

Having joined the grammar school, it became apparent to Joyce that most of the other pupils came from affluent backgrounds, despite the school being located in one of the poorest areas of Glasgow. As she took the two buses to and from school, she observed the street scenes, working out the gulf between the 'haves' and 'have nots'. As a student she excelled in art and music but was hopeless at maths, gravely disappointing her father, who otherwise would have steered her towards accountancy. Her brother Brian went to Glasgow High School, but her youngest brother, David, developed epilepsy when he was about eight years old. His mother constantly worried about him, sending him to the local school in Bellahouston, where she could keep a closer eye on him.

About two years after the memorable Beatles concert, Joyce had a discussion with her father about her future. George recommended she apply for a university place, but his daughter was at the rebellious age with an independent spirit. Joyce wanted to study at art college, preferably in London, which apparently was 'swinging'. George had no intention of allowing such a thing, preferring to ease her through Scottish Highers and direct her towards training as a librarian. Joyce had always been a keen reader, and now had access to books from every genre. She was particularly drawn to detective novels, devouring titles by Agatha Christie and Dorothy L. Sayers. But the shift pattern was disruptive to her social life and when after six months she could no longer bear to work alongside the librarian – an elderly spinster with attitude – she resigned, and joined the National Savings Bank as a clerical officer.

It was a job. At least the regular hours meant evenings out with her girlfriends, enjoying live music in the pubs of Glasgow. She found herself attracted to a young musician called Tony, a guitarist in a group. Her new boyfriend's day job was as a metalworker in the shipyards. Despite Tony not meeting with George's approval, he realised he had little choice and agreed to give his daughter away at a traditional white wedding. The situation took a turn for the worse when Tony lost his job and was unable to find another. However, his uncle lived 'down south', somewhere called Norwich, working for Boulton & Paul, a major city engineering company that was taking on trained tradesman. In 1972, Joyce found herself transplanted into a different world. Just after her arrival in the city, Joyce was sent for a chest X-ray, suffering with suspected pleurisy. No one, not even Joyce, was aware that she was newly pregnant and sadly the procedure proved fatal for the baby. At full term, the baby was stillborn with spina bifida and hydrocephalus. Joyce and Tony were never offered the chance to see their son.

Understandably shocked, Tony began hiding all the baby clothes and equipment they had bought during the pregnancy. He could not prevent Joyce disintegrating into months of postnatal depression, buoyed up with prescription pills and counselling sessions. Once recovered enough to work, Joyce found herself a job at Reckitt & Colman. She operated a massive machine, controlling and monitoring the movement of wooden pallets up and down the country, stacked high with jars of mustard or empty and ready for loading. Two years later, in February 1974, Joyce gave birth to a healthy son, and they named him Ross. While the young couple were settling into parenthood, they learnt that the Labour-led Norwich City Council, from which they had received an improvement grant for their first home in Rosary Road, had now placed the house on the list for demolition. The couple felt most aggrieved. They found a new home at the top of Thunder Lane in the attractive suburb of Thorpe St Andrew.

Two further babies followed, Jennifer and Alistair. Joyce was a stalwart of the local mother and toddler groups and National Childbirth Trust. When she needed more adult company she joined the ladies' darts team at the Artichoke pub in Magdalen Road. Meanwhile, Tony's horizons were broadening; he was now working on gas and oil projects, travelling overseas often for three weeks at a time. Joyce struggled on alone, helped enormously by Tony's sister Margaret and her husband, recently moved down from Scotland. With no children of their own, the couple enjoyed being the attentive auntie and uncle. When Tony was at home, Joyce sensed a distance developing between him and the family. It was as if he were holding them at arm's length. In 1989, an opportunity arose for him to visit factories in Bulgaria, setting up freezer systems. The company supplied him with a female interpreter who in time 'turned his head'. With his wife recovering from an operation in hospital, Tony could not cope with the developing situation and just walked away. Joyce was forty years old; they had been married for eighteen years. The family was heartbroken. A few months later, Joyce's father died. It had been a dreadful year.

With mortgage payments in arrears, Joyce lost her family home in Thorpe St Andrew. For a while she rented an old property in St Williams Way, where the boys slept alongside a giant cheese plant, left behind by the previous tenants. The carpets were disgusting and every door had been kicked in. But the children loved it, especially the extensive garden. When the landlord put the house up for sale, Joyce had no choice but to apply to the Council, living in a series of houses in Heartsease and Sprowston. Once Ross and Jennifer had left home, she took a tiny flat in Ebenezer Place in the city centre. Despite having very little money, it never occurred to Joyce to claim benefits; she just kept on working.

There were three very different activities that saved her sanity, particularly when times were tough: art, local politics and Morris dancing. She joined a group of female dancers known as Fiddlesticks North West Clog. Dressed in green skirts and black waistcoats, the ladies danced outside pubs and on village greens to live accompaniment of a concertina, tin whistle, fiddle and drums. It was great fun. But most important to Joyce was her art. She had never lost her desire to have formal training. For years she repeatedly applied to Norwich School of Art, and was disappointed never to receive an offer. With no intention of giving up, she identified a similar course at the College of Art and Design in Great Yarmouth, where she was accepted as a mature student. It was tough but exhilarating, and at the end of four years she was awarded a Higher Diploma. But with three school-aged children to clothe and feed, her dream of living as a professional artist was simply impossible. Her new qualification meant she could apply for the role of Creative Activity Co-ordinator with Social Services, working for Norfolk County Council, based at the Copper Kettle Day Centre for people with mental health problems. Further assignments included working as a craft instructor with dementia patients in care homes, including at Burlingham House, a prestigious care home on the edge of the Norfolk Broads.

Although never considering local politics before, in 2000 she was persuaded to join a group of Lib Dem activists, led by Philip Moore and Brian Watkins, delivering campaign leaflets around neighbouring streets. Over time Joyce became increasingly involved, making new friends and feeling valued and productive. A year later, Joyce felt ready to stand as a councillor, along with her friend Samantha Allison, for the Liberal Democrat ward of Thorpe Hamlet, both ladies winning a seat. During her first year, Joyce felt her way, encouraged by the rise in popularity of the Liberal Democrat group. It began to look as if they just might win a majority in the 2002 elections. With this in mind, Joyce reduced her hours with Social Services to three days a week. In 2002, the dream became a reality, with Derek Wood becoming the first Liberal Democrat Lord Mayor to hold office while in power.

The following year, Lib Dem Chris Southgate took the role, but by early 2004 it was proving a challenge to identify someone within the group who either had the time or the inclination to be Lord Mayor. Councillor Felicity Hartley was asked, but she could not guarantee to be available, being responsible for her Down's syndrome son Christopher. Ian Couzens, Leader of the Council, approached Joyce, surprising her with the offer. She had only been a councillor for three years. Could she come back to him? She needed to talk it over with Alistair.

Joyce had first met Alistair Pitty in September 1995 at the Fat Cat, a popular real ale pub in the city. He was a fellow Scot and she enjoyed talking to him. Over the next few weeks they continually kept bumping into each other, most notably at a ballroom dancing club open night, and later as fellow guests at a dinner party hosted by a mutual friend. Alistair, ten years her senior, was an independent consultant specialising in a strand of geology. Recently divorced, he owned a home in Norwich. There didn't seem any harm in sharing the odd pint while listening to live folk music. Their relationship developed and once Joyce's youngest son had left home for art college, the couple moved in together, buying a Victorian home in Telegraph Lane East, in Joyce's own ward of Thorpe Hamlet.

Joyce accepted the nomination. Alistair would, of course, be supportive, and agreed to be her official consort. In 2004, the local elections were delayed until 10 June, to coincide with the European Elections. Joyce and her two colleagues, Samantha Allison and Jill Surridge, swept the board in Thorpe Hamlet, the Liberal Democrat group holding the majority of seats with eighteen, but they had lost overall control. Labour won fifteen seats and the Green Party took five, effectively holding the balance of power in any crucial votes. The Green Party Leader, 22-year-old student Adrian Ramsay, was hailed in the press as a rising star of local politics. Only one Conservative councillor was returned, Evelyn Collishaw, her time as Lord Mayor still five years away.

Mayor-Making, despite being officially the annual meeting of the Council, is traditionally non-political, held almost exclusively to induct the new Lord Mayor and Sheriff. But on 29 June, the tradition and ceremony was overshadowed by a controversial row in the Chamber, led by the new body of Green councillors. Joyce, resplendent in the black and gold robe, had been sworn in as Lord Mayor and the new Sheriff, Paul King, was wearing the ancient chain. Relatives and visitors high above in the public gallery were taken aback by an unexpected political debate developing in front of them. Joyce was now officially chairing the meeting – her first time in the big canopied chair complete with cushion to raise her into view – expecting to have a report on a best-value performance plan go through 'on the nod'. But two newly elected Green councillors were having none of it and were raising concerns, specifically on transport and recycling issues. Labour Councillor Nick Williams argued that the annual meeting was not the right time to talk politics. Joyce took this as her cue, putting the issue to the vote, so calling a halt to further disruption. The civic group were forty minutes behind schedule when they gathered for photographs on City Hall steps.

Having a Lord Mayor who works on three days a week creates havoc with the civic diary. Fortunately, her Civic Secretary, Heather Ashmore, was an experienced officer, taking it all in her stride, while Sheriff Paul King, a local businessman and stalwart of the Norwich Society, proved an admirable stand-in when required. Paul was also very handy with a camera, taking photos at functions, the results being usually more candid than those of the official photographer. Alistair was a great support, despite his own work responsibilities, never letting Joyce down. He was also an accomplished speechwriter, and the two of them spent many evenings burning the midnight oil as they worked on the next script.

Of all the official engagements undertaken by Joyce that year, four in particular stand out. At her Civic Service at Norwich Cathedral, the procession included the colourful and ebullient Norwich Whifflers and Snap the Dragon, the first time they had accompanied a female Lord Mayor after their revival in 1996.[2] Joyce was always pleased to see them at events, especially as traditionally Snap is said to protect the Lord Mayor from evil spirits! On 30 August 1944, the French city of Rouen was liberated from the Nazis by Canadian troops. Rouen was twinned with Norwich in 1959, and in August 2004, Joyce was invited to attend the sixtieth anniversary celebrations of liberation. Joyce and Alistair could hardly believe the welcome they received, as they were driven from the airport in a black limousine with police outriders and passed down the grand Avenue de la Libération, with lines of veterans marching past and waving the Tricolore. On arrival at their five-star hotel, they were thrilled to discover floral bouquets, complimentary wine and chocolates. At the champagne reception and seven-course lunch, Joyce was seated next to a charming French Canadian Army officer, a welcome distraction as she nervously awaited her moment to read her speech in French. But she and Alistair had triple-checked the text and rehearsed it over and over. Joyce was relieved to get through it without too much sniggering from the locals!

In July 2004, the government announced large cuts in the armed forces as part of modernisation plans. One casualty was HMS *Norfolk*, the sixth Royal Navy frigate to be so named, launched on the Clyde by Princess Margaret in July 1987. The ship would be decommissioned in April 2005, but was scheduled to sail up the Thames for the last time in November 2004. On the invitation list to join the ship for this voyage were the Lord Mayor of Norwich and her consort, the Chairman of Norfolk County Council and his wife, and, unusually, Civic Secretary Heather, along with Pauline, her opposite number at County Hall. It was very early in the morning when the intrepid six met to be equipped with red survival suits and lifejackets in preparation for the short helicopter ride to the ship, sailing just off Great Yarmouth and heading for the mouth of the Thames. As County Hall staff began arriving for work, while the group was still waiting by the rear entrance, one asked anxiously: 'Has there been a chemical incident?'

Adrenaline levels rose as they heard the sound of whirring blades. Joyce was nervous about the take-off, later likening it to 'going up in a lift'. The North Sea was grey and forbidding, but every passenger made it safely to the deck of the moving ship, removing their survival suits before being treated to a traditional English breakfast at the captain's table. The ship made its way past familiar landmarks through choppy waters, sailing towards somber inky clouds hanging over the city of London. On the drive home to Norwich, the team relaxed in the civic limousine, all agreeing that it had been a fantastic experience.[3]

In May 2005, Joyce handed the mantle to Labour Councillor Michael Banham.

She described her mayoral year as having been a tremendous privilege and an amazing experience, adding: 'Everyone is always pleased to see you. Unlike when you are a councillor knocking on the door, when they don't want to see you.' Joyce continued to represent the people of Thorpe Hamlet, holding her seat in 2006, despite Labour taking control of the city. She remained loyal until May 2010, when she stood down in protest at the coalition government's withdrawal of restructuring plans for Norwich City Council.

Following her retirement from Social Services in April 2013, Joyce now volunteers as an Appropriate Adult, helping vulnerable people held for questioning by the police in one of four custody suites in Norfolk. Occasionally she is called out to the Norvic Clinic, a high security unit in Thorpe St Andrew for people with mental illness who have broken the law. She loves rambling, most recently Nordic Walking, she sketches and paints whenever she can, and regularly returns to Scotland with Alistair to visit her mum. Grandchildren now feature in her life; her only sadness is that her daughter Jenny, a professional punk musician with an extensive international career behind her, now lives in Australia with her husband and young son Lochland. They keep in touch through the use of Skype calls. Joyce's son Ross lives in Norwich with his two girls, Kiera and Lauren, conveniently close to enjoy special 'Grandma time', whilst youngest son Alistair lives in London, working for international fragrance entrepreneur Jo Malone. Joyce remains an enthusiastic member of the local Liberal Democrats, supporting fundraising events whenever possible.

Joyce still remembers with a sense of glee the day in 2004 when she witnessed the stonemason engraving her name into the marble slab outside the Council Chamber. She had requested that both her married and maiden name be included. 'That was an amazing moment. You look at that great scroll of names going *way* back and you think, "My name is on there." I can't believe I did it now!'

Endnotes

1. Robert Climie died aged sixty-one of a 'severe internal malady' in the Victoria Infirmary Glasgow, just five months after his re-election on 3 October 1929.

2. In years gone by, the whifflers were officers who walked in front of processions to clear the way for the monarch or the mayor, blowing a horn and carrying swords. Later these brightly coloured characters became a major part of the Mayor-Making ceremony. However, with the Municipal Corporation Act of 1835, the feasting and revelry that accompanied the annual installation of a city mayor was stopped. In 1996, a local group of Morris dancers, Kemps Men of Norwich, supported by the Norwich Society, resurrected the tradition and have appeared at important civic events ever since. They are usually accompanied by Snap the Dragon, a large puppet and a relic of the days of the Guild of St George. Snap represents misrule and evil. He is not allowed to enter sacred places but each year attempts to enter Norwich Cathedral and is repulsed by the Bishop.

3. HMS *Norfolk* was sold to the Chilean Navy in 2006.

Joyce Anthea Climie Divers 2004–2005

Further Highlights from her Mayoral Year

- Presenting the Freedom of the City of Norwich to Sir Timothy Colman in the company of the Vice Chancellor of UEA and Chairman of Norfolk County Council.

- Meeting the Prince of Wales at the Royal Norfolk Show, with him likening Alistair to Denis Thatcher.

- Managing not to fall over as she walked backwards in high heels from laying the civic wreath on Remembrance Sunday.

- Raising £23,024 for Assist Trust, a Norwich-based charity offering independence programmes for people with learning difficulties.

- Presenting two national swimming awards to Norwich Swan Swimming Club during a gala at the UEA Sportspark.

- Unveiling a memorial at Norwich Airport, to American servicemen killed in Norfolk in the Second World War.

- Representing Norwich in Leeds at the Anglia in Bloom Awards.

- Joining old friends from Fiddlesticks North West Clog troop as they danced outside Norwich Cathedral.

- Visiting the twinned town of Koblenz with the Norwich Philharmonic Choir and being presented with a souvenir umbrella at the after-concert reception, which proved invaluable on a very wet visit to the castle the following day.

- Accepting an invitation from the Lord Mayor of Oxford to visit the city and take a tour of Brasenose College, where Alistair studied for his degree.

- Celebrating the promotion of Norwich City Football Club to the Premier League after nine years in the First Division. Seeing the enormous inflatable yellow canary tethered to the roof of City Hall.

- Riding into Cathedral Close inside the civic coach.

- Attending an event held by Assist Trust, a charity that helps people with learning difficulties progress and move forward with their lives.

CHAPTER 12

Felicity Hartley
(1945–)

Lord Mayor of Norwich 2006–2007

I remember when we met the Catholic Bishop of East Anglia, Michael Evans. I turned around and saw Chris marching up to him, holding out his hand. 'My mother is the Lord Mayor and I am her consort. How do you do?' Michael was lovely. He replied, 'I know, and I'm the Bishop.' Bishop Graham always made us very welcome, inviting us to a garden party in the Bishop's garden. Chris was socially very confident by the end of the year. I think the whole experience did him an enormous amount of good.

(Felicity Hartley, speaking in 2016)

Unusually, the inauguration of the twelfth lady Lord Mayor of Norwich was captured on film.[1] The opening frames show a silver-haired woman emerging from a taxi at the foot of City Hall steps. A stocky young man with a chopped fringe and dark-rimmed spectacles takes her arm and escorts her up the stone steps to the brass-fronted doors. That morning, Tuesday, 23 May 2006, Felicity Hartley, Liberal Democrat Councillor for Town Close Ward, woke suffering the nerves of a bride-to-be. For today was Mayor-Making, and Christopher, her 26-year-old son, was to be her official consort.

Heeding advice about the heavy chain, Felicity had spent the past three months scouring the local charity shops for jackets with padded shoulders. She pragmatically decided on comfortable kitten heels, buying at least two pairs. With May approaching it was time to speak to City Hall about her choice of official consort. Having been divorced for fifteen years, with no current 'significant other' in her life, Felicity had spent many nights considering this decision. She had three grown-up sons. Brendan was away travelling, and eldest Adrian was married and living in London. This left middle son, Christopher. Felicity approached the Chief Executive. 'Christopher has Down's syndrome – will that give the Council a problem?'

At the outbreak of war in September 1939, Percy Kenneth Watkins (he preferred 'Ken') and Margery Butterworth had been engaged for four years. Margery presented her solicitor fiancé with an ultimatum: 'If you're planning to join up then there must be a wedding before you leave home.' The couple married and Ken spent the next six years in the Army, serving mainly overseas. Margery was the daughter of a Lancashire-born trader on the Cotton Exchange in Liverpool, and the family were members of the Liberal Party. Ken's father, the proprietor of two 'posh' grocer's shops, was a stalwart of the opposing Conservative tradition. In October 1944, Ken took two days' leave to spend in London with his wife. That night the couple were woken by a flying bomb, resulting nine months later in the birth of their daughter Felicity, on 13 July 1945.

Ten years on, Ken joined a firm of solicitors in Southport, gaining a reputation as a skilled orator in court. His next move was to the Prosecutions Department in Bradford, living on the wild and picturesque Ilkley Moor. Having loved the natural landscape, at nine years old Felicity was dismayed when her father uprooted them again, this time relocating 'down south' to Chelmsford as a prosecutor for Essex County Council. At eleven, Felicity joined the prestigious Chelmsford County High School for Girls, where the students were encouraged to be independent and informed about national and global issues. On a school trip to Central Hall, Westminster, Felicity heard the young Shirley Williams MP speaking at a meeting of the Council for Education and World Citizenship. In 1964, Felicity, a conscientious student, was offered a place to read English and Literature at Durham University, where she joined others in the student's union, hearing well-known guest speakers, including the outspoken Conservative MP Enoch Powell.

During the 1960s, County Durham was predominantly a mining community with working pits in many villages. The hardships suffered by many of the miners and their families affected Felicity profoundly, steering her towards socialist politics. Having graduated, she spent a brief spell working in London, before returning to Durham to take up an administrative role at the university. When one of her former lecturers stood as a Labour MP, Felicity joined his team, gaining an insight into grass roots politics. Having voted Labour in the 1970 general election, her allegiance shifted towards the Liberal Party. She was particularly influenced by the Poulson Affair in 1974[2] and the corruption scandal surrounding former Leader of Newcastle Council, T. Dan Smith.[3]

In 1974 she secured the post of Senior Administrative Assistant in the Personnel Department at the University of East Anglia in Norwich, arriving on New Year's Day 1975 knowing only one person in the city. Anxious to establish a social life, within four days she was scouring the *Evening News* for inspiration. A classical guitar concert by the well-known Paco Peña at the Assembly House caught her eye. Arriving at the venue, Felicity was shocked to discover that the concert had been moved to Blackfriars Hall. Not knowing where to find the new location, she asked for directions from another misplaced audience member. They walked across the city together, her new friend later inviting Felicity to join her for a drink at the Bystanders Society on Thorpe Road. This popular and active social club, opened in 1959, was to become a lifeline, with its ambitious programme of themed meals, treasure hunts, outings, beer festivals and amateur theatre productions.

Anxious to buy a property, Felicity took advantage of the 100 per cent mortgage offer from Norwich City Council, an initiative led by Labour Councillor Patricia Hollis, the future Baroness Hollis of Heigham. Felicity soon moved into a modest house on Beaumont Place. It was now that two men entered her life: firstly David Seelhoff, an electronics engineer in the North Sea oil industry; and the other, John Hartley, the son of Eric and Freda Hartley, a well-known political couple in the city.[4] Although attracted to both men, John's situation was complicated. His permanent home was in Rhodesia, a country in the grip of civil war. Felicity was unwilling to leave her ailing father for an uncertain future in such a volatile environment. John returned to Africa and Felicity became Mrs Seelhoff in the autumn of 1976. Eighteen months later, their first son, Adrian Charles, was born. The families were delighted.

On 26 February 1980, a second son arrived. But Christopher Luke was different. Their baby had a genetic disorder, which was at that time called Mongolism and is now known as Down's syndrome. Felicity was thirty-four years old. Whilst she was aware of the potential consequences, David's reaction was one of shock and profound disappointment. Uncertain of the future, David questioned the validity of taking the baby home. But as Felicity bonded with the infant, she knew that giving up her son was simply not an option. Several conversations with professionals followed, with David finally acquiescing. Baby Christopher joined 2-year-old Adrian in the family home in Poringland. David remained sceptical and the couple's marriage came under immense strain.

It was a challenging time. Christopher had difficulty feeding, being reluctant to move on from bottles to solids. He was in and out of hospital, and unable to walk until he was nearly four years old. Felicity was impressed by the excellent care and support they received from health visitors, paediatricians and social workers who introduced her to parents in a similar position, enabling her to glean invaluable first-hand advice. Felicity and David together made a conscious decision to try again for another baby, and she fell pregnant almost immediately. Their third son, Brendan Kenneth, arrived at the end of 1981. Felicity was philosophical, bringing up her two younger boys as if they were twins, with two high chairs, spoon-feeding them side by side.

David was away working much of the time. When he was home he endeavoured to be a good father to his three boys, but was still uncomfortable around Christopher. David suffered episodes of depression, and the situation was exacerbated by Felicity losing both her parents within two years of each other. Margery succumbed to cancer aged seventy-one in June 1982, followed by Ken dying in a Norwich nursing home in February 1984, aged seventy-six, having suffered from a form of multiple sclerosis for some years. Felicity's inheritance offered financial independence and she secured the money away for her future. Felicity and David divorced in 1991. By this time Felicity and John were back in touch, tentatively talking about a possible future together.

Felicity bought a three-bedroomed semi in Town Close, moving in with her three sons. Before long, wedding plans were under way, with Felicity and John looking forward to a future together as a family. However, in September 1991, while helping with the chores, John collapsed with heart failure onto Felicity's kitchen floor. He was forty-nine years old. Felicity was devastated:

> This was so unfair. Although my life had been completely turned upside down, the one thing I was not going to do was to fall apart. I would make a good job of the rest of my life. John had put me back in touch with myself and back on track somehow.[5]

Her friendship with John's parents grew even closer, and in memory of John, Felicity changed her name by deed poll to Hartley.

Heartbroken and anxious about coping as a single mother, Felicity withdrew and considered her options. One evening in the mid-1990s, a Liberal Democrat activist, Brian Watkins,[6] knocked on her door in Cecil Road. On discovering the occupant was already a card-carrying member, he pushed a little harder, and the resulting conversation proved advantageous for Norwich South branch. Felicity was persuaded to once again become involved with the now rebranded Liberal Democrats. This decision would lead to her representing the Down's Syndrome Norfolk Support Group on the former Norwich Community Health Council, later becoming Chairman of the Mental Health Group.

By 1998, Christopher was eighteen and in his final year at Harford Manor School for children with complex needs. Adrian was at university and Brendan still at school. Turning down the offer to stand as a county councillor, wary of the notoriously heavy workload, Felicity reasoned that she might manage a seat on Norwich City Council. The party offered her a chance to stand in Town Close Ward, her home patch and at that time a Liberal Democrat stronghold. With growing enthusiasm, she worked hard, knocking on doors, canvassing, delivering leaflets and talking to the residents about their concerns. Her reward was a comfortable win. The overall election results for the Liberal Democrats were encouraging. Having worked in academia and being no stranger to working with committees, Felicity felt at ease in the Council Chamber, alongside forty-seven councillors, eleven of whom were Liberal Democrats.

Christopher moved out of the home, first as a weekly boarder at the College of West Anglia near King's Lynn, and later into supported living placements. Most weekends he went home to be with his mum. Brendan left for university, allowing Felicity to concentrate on being a hands-on councillor. She was indebted to John's parents, who enjoyed offering her advice on the rigours of council work. At the 2001 elections the Liberal Democrats unexpectedly took Lakenham, which had been until then a strong Labour ward. This was most encouraging.

At the May elections of 2002, the Liberal Democrat group finally gained control of Norwich City Council, after virtually seventy years of uninterrupted Labour dominance.[7] Felicity, although tempted to stand as Lord Mayor, was still constantly 'on call' in case Christopher had problems at college. She simply could not take the risk. Over the following months, galvanised by the additional responsibilities of power, Felicity took on the Culture and Arts Portfolio, securing the future of Norwich Playhouse, which had been under financial threat for some time. But with increasing budget difficulties and the rise in popularity of the Green Party, within two years the political scene was changing. The election of 2004 saw Norwich with no overall control, although the Liberal Democrats still held the majority of seats. By the end of 2005, Felicity could sense that the following year might possibly be her last chance. In January she won the nomination. She set about preparing to visit son Brendan, who was travelling in Australia, confident that whatever the decision of the Norwich electors, she would be Lord Mayor by the summer.

'If you had told me thirty years ago that I would be standing here wearing bling that would make Victoria Beckham green with envy, I would have said you were mad!' It was quite an opening to her Mayor-Making ceremony, and one that was appreciated by the audience. Felicity thanked her sons, her colleagues from Norwich Soroptimists group, close friends Margaret and June, who had travelled down from Yorkshire, and her Norwich pals in the LPU,[8] and, finally, paid tribute to Eric and Freda Hartley. Christopher had sat patiently throughout, waiting to receive his official consort's badge. He was to be the first person with Down's syndrome to be so honoured. It was a proud moment when the ribbon was placed around his neck. Felicity's only sadness was that the Liberal Democrat group had indeed lost control of the Council only a few days earlier. Felicity spoke again that evening, in the Rotunda of Norwich Castle – the traditional venue for the 'At Home' event. Within half an hour of arriving at her house, Felicity was curled up asleep on the living room floor, when supposed to be hosting a family 'carpet picnic'. It had been a long day.

And so began Felicity's twelve months as First Citizen. She became renowned for her eloquent speeches, a skill most likely inherited from her father. Council budget cuts meant Felicity had to hire taxis to events deep in the countryside, often at weekends. She dug in her heels, asking how it would look if the Lord Mayor got lost and arrived shattered and frazzled. She would have custody of an antique chain worth thousands of pounds, but what about security? A permanent solution was eventually found midway through Felicity's civic year, when Gavin Thorpe, a retired Norwich fire fighter, was employed as Civic Attendant, Sword Bearer and Driver. He and Christopher shared many amusing moments during their car journeys.

The local press actively featured articles about this fascinating mother and son team. The local support organisation Down's Syndrome

Norfolk, of which Felicity is a founder member, published an interview in the summer edition of the members' newsletter. When asked what they were both looking forward to the most, Felicity replied, 'the street procession', whereas Christopher focused on one of his favourite spectator sports, confidently stating, 'I am looking forward to the football!' The official civic charity for 2006 was BREAK, a Norfolk-based organisation helping vulnerable young people, its mission to 'provide services of the highest quality, working together to create stability and improve opportunities for a better future'. Felicity knew first-hand how much their work benefitted families such as hers, delighted to be able to present to them a cheque for £18,000 at the end of her year. Felicity and Chris were invited to many events held by mental health and disabled charities. Felicity later reflected, 'Chris was happy with this, but by and large he preferred mainstream events where there was good food and pretty girls – like most young men of his age!' It was often noted that at certain functions, Chris would begin to lose interest, openly stating, 'Mum, I'm bored now, time to go home.' But Felicity might not yet have given her speech!

Felicity approached her civic role as she had parenthood, benefitting from her experience as a mother of three sons:

> With boys you find yourself unimpressed when they play up. And men in politics can act exactly like 10-year-old boys in a strop. With some you can rely on the inbuilt respect for their mother and with others it is a matter of thinking, 'I'm not having that!'

By the end of May 2007, Felicity's boxes of cuttings and photographs were overflowing. Labour Councillor Roy Blower, a popular figure in the city with his close associations to the Norwich City Football Club, was Lord Mayor elect. Gavin Thorpe recalls the scene in the Council Chamber:

> Christopher was the outgoing consort. My role was to de-invest him. I was a little nervous about how he might take this but as I lifted the badge over his head, he looked at me and grinned, throwing his arms around me! That went down a storm. It was quite an emotional moment. We had a hug in the middle of the Council Chamber in the middle of Mayor-Making.

Felicity stood down as a councillor in 2008, ready to take on different challenges. The following years brought family change, with 2012 proving particularly momentous. With only weeks until Felicity was due to fly to Canada to meet the Bangladeshi parents of son Adrian's fiancée, he called to say that his father had broken his leg and was in the Norfolk and Norwich Hospital. David had been due to take Christopher to the London Olympics the following day. Rather than have him miss this special treat, Felicity arranged for a carer to take him instead, after which she paid a visit to the hospital. On the way home Adrian made the surprise announcement that the gathering in Canada was, in fact, to be his wedding. The following day, David had a sudden embolism and by the afternoon he had died. Felicity and her sons were in shock. Almost before the news had properly sunk in, Felicity and Adrian flew out for the Muslim marriage ceremony, returning promptly to England for David's funeral.

Felicity's relationship with her boys remains strong. Brendan and wife Sian presented the family with Jack, Felicity's first grandchild, in 2015. Christopher lives in a supported living bungalow in Costessey, attending Sprowston Day Services and Thalia Theatre, enjoying craft activities, rehearsals and performances held in St Saviour's Church in Magdalen Street. His mum looks forward to his weekends at home. She continues as an active member of the Norwich Soroptimists and has fun with the ladies of the Red Hat Society. Established in 2006 and inspired by a poem by Jenny Joseph called *When I am Old*, members of this national organisation for ladies of 'a certain age' wear purple dresses and red hats, attracting smiles everywhere they go.

In an article for *Councillor Magazine*, given shortly after her civic year, Felicity said of her middle son:

> Chris soon picked up one of the main requirements of the role – which is to smile and be friendly; both things come naturally to him. Parents of disabled children have come up to me and said how good it is to see Chris carrying out this role. It was a bit of a gamble but we have met loads of new people and raised the profile of those with learning difficulties, showing they can play a real part in public life – that is all I hoped for.

Endnotes

1. Eastern Associates, Norfolk 2006.
2. John Poulson was a prominent architect, jailed for five years for corruption, and found guilty of bribing public figures to win contracts. He denied all charges.

3. T. Dan Smith was jailed for pocketing cash and passing on bribes.
4. The couple became Lord Mayor and Lady Mayoress of Norwich in 1980.
5. Felicity Hartley, speaking in 2016.
6. Sheriff of Norwich, in 1990.
7. The Conservative Group took control during the period 1968–70, when Labour Prime Minister Harold Wilson was introducing unpopular economic measures.
8. Ladies' Piss-Up is a group of friends who regularly meet at each other's homes on Tuesday lunchtimes.

Felicity Hartley 2006–2007

Further Highlights from her Mayoral Year

- Arriving with Christopher in the civic coach for the Civic Service at Norwich Cathedral and reading a bible passage from Revelations 21.

- Welcoming the annual conference of the National Association of City and Town Sheriffs to Norwich, and leading them in a procession, accompanied by the Norwich Whifflers and Snap the Dragon.

- Attending the EAST International Exhibition of Contemporary Art at Norwich School of Art and being presented with a cloth carrier bag emblazoned with a photograph of herself as Lord Mayor, featuring her wide smile and feathered hat.

- Riding in an open-topped Datsun with Christopher in the Lord Mayor's Parade, followed by fifty-five floats and bands. Waving at the hundreds of people lining the route through the city. It was one of Christopher's favourite events.

- Being photographed in a group of academics including Sir Robert Winston during a graduation ceremony at the University of East Anglia.

- Welcoming the public into the Lord Mayor's Parlour on Heritage Open Day.

- Awarding the Freedom of the City to 73-year-old Swedish speedway star Ove Fundin, a key member of Norwich Stars from 1955 to 1964, winning five world titles. Being photographed astride a speedway bike wearing the black and gold robe.

- Seeing the Spitfire Flypast over City Hall during the Battle of Britain Week opening ceremony.

- Being driven in a dodgem car by the Bishop of Lynn, James Langstaff, at the King's Lynn Mart.

- Meeting Sir Bobby Robson at a local derby match, Ipswich vs Norwich City. Ipswich won 3–1.

- Welcoming the medieval gold Loving Cup as part of its national tour to celebrate St George's Day.

- Celebrating the Civic Sisterhood Event – the 100th anniversary celebration of women first being allowed to stand as candidates in local council elections. Being joined by more than fifty female councillors, both past and present, including Baroness Patricia Hollis and Past Lord Mayors of Norwich Jill Miller, Brenda Ferris and Joyce Divers.

CHAPTER 13

Evelyn Jean Collishaw
(1945–)

Lord Mayor of Norwich 2009–10

I became a 'Ten Pound Pom', travelling to Australia by sea. Mind you, I thought it would be more of a luxury cruise! It turned out to be not great. There were eight of us in a cabin, just like school dorms. I had never been on a ship before. Luckily I was only a little bit seasick but some people were seasick the whole time. It was an Italian ship with a Chinese crew. It took a month to get there. I thought, 'We'll see the Pyramids, we'll see all these things,' but of course we didn't stop. We went through the Suez Canal and the first stop was Aden to refuel. It was 110 degrees, which I had not experienced before. There were lots of Arabs trying to sell us fake gold watches and dirty postcards.

(Eve Collishaw, speaking in 2016)

As a young woman Evelyn Collishaw had a quest to see the world. In 1966 she shocked friends by resigning from a dream job at Anglia Television. She had been Assistant to the Company Secretary, working at its studios in the old Agricultural Hall alongside legendary news presenter Dick Joice and socialising with the emerging television stars of the future. But since 1945, the Government of Australia had been orchestrating one of the largest planned mass migrations of the twentieth century, offering a crossing for just £10 to this burgeoning land of sun and opportunity. An interview at the Australian Embassy in London explained that migrants had to stay for at least two years, or pay back the full fare, which was more than ten times the price on offer. Eve took the risk, and at twenty-one began her adventure.

It took some time to reach Australia; the ship had been involved in a horrendous typhoon in the Indian Ocean before docking at Perth, a town still in its infancy, and then sailing on to Melbourne, arriving late on a Saturday afternoon. The young passengers were disappointed to find that the pubs closed at the ridiculously early hour of 8.00 pm. Eve was so disgusted with Melbourne that she never returned. Once in Sydney, Eve set up home with two of her fellow travellers, enjoying the novelties of hamburgers, smoothies and cheap wine. But women were not tolerated in Australian bars, still being considered as inferior. Eve found a job with Australian broadcaster Channel 10. She travelled to work on the ferry across Sydney harbour amongst commuters intrigued by the army of labourers building the controversial Opera House. She was resident in the city for three years, taking time out to visit Queensland, trying opal digging and gold panning, and experiencing the magnificent Barrier Reef.

Eve returned to Norwich in 1969. She helped to set up the Manpower Recruitment Office, but found it difficult to settle down. Early in 1970, she travelled to South Africa, where, for six months, she helped establish an architects' practice in Cape Town. But despite enjoying her job and making good friends, the Apartheid laws made Eve feel profoundly uncomfortable; it was time to move on. She knew of relatives from Scotland who had emigrated to Southern Rhodesia[1] and she set out to find them, taking a long-distance train journey through Botswana, being fascinated by the landscape unfolding before her. Rhodesia was a wealthy British colony, governed since 1964 by politician, farmer and former fighter pilot Ian Smith. Life here was more relaxed than in South Africa. Having found her relations – a surgeon and his family – in the capital Salisbury, she stayed, and worked for a mining company. Back home, Eve's father, Edward Roy Collishaw, was diagnosed with a brain tumour and was admitted to Addenbrooke's Hospital in Cambridge. His condition deteriorated and in June 1971 Eve was summoned to return home. She did not hesitate, and boarded a plane for London. By the time she was at his bedside, 59-year-old Edward was unconscious. She had arrived just too late to say goodbye.

Edward's family was originally from Lincolnshire, and during the mid-1930s he was working as a pharmacist in Boots the Chemist in the market town of Oundle, 15 miles south-west of Peterborough. Quite by chance he met a young woman, recently moved into the area from the Clyde Valley in Lanarkshire. Edward was thirty and Matilda Campbell Miller five years younger. They were married in Scotland in 1940. No one is sure why Edward Roy did not join the armed forces during the war. His poor eyesight may have been the issue, or as a pharmacist, his occupation may have been reserved. Whatever the reason, unlike his younger brother Alan, who joined the RAF, he took a job at Reads Pharmacy on Magdalen Road in Norwich. He would work there for more than thirty years, and was known by the locals as 'Mr Read'. Eve never knew her paternal grandfather Edward, a retired wheelwright, as he died in 1943, two years before she was born. But she is proud to have been named after her grandmother, a woman whose tenacity she much admired. Grandmother Evelyn had lost both her parents by twenty-eight years old, raised three children and lived to be ninety.

Edward and Matilda's first baby was a son, Edward Bryce, born in November 1943, followed by Evelyn Jean on 3 April 1945, just a month before the end of hostilities in Europe. Norwich was a city disfigured by bomb damage. Matilda later told tales of pushing baby Bryce in his pram up Mousehold Avenue, looking down on the city and watching the fires burning below. Matilda enjoyed visiting the airfields with the good ladies of the WRVS, taking tea and buns to the American airmen, once taking to the skies on a joy ride! The family lived in the flat above the chemist's shop, but in 1946, with his business doing well, Edward Roy bought a house at 42 Constitution Hill. With its corner plot overlooking Sewell Park, square bays and oval portico, this solidly built Edwardian family home better reflected his status as a professional man.

As a young girl Eve loved to join her father in the back room of the shop, 'helping' to mix potions and wrap pills into brown paper parcels. Shop assistant Hilary[2] encouraged young Evelyn to make crêpe paper roses to enhance the flasks of brightly coloured water displayed in the window. At eleven, Eve joined Norwich High School for Girls, cycling the 4 miles across the city to Newmarket Road. When his daughter chose science subjects at 'A' level, Edward Roy encouraged Eve to follow him into pharmacy. But she had lost her earlier enthusiasm for pills and potions, instead convincing her father to pay for a business course at a secretarial college in London, where she gained skills that in time would pay her way around the world. Her brother Bryce, however, delighted his father by training for the profession, eventually running several shops and retaining the name Reads Chemists. Eve's father was successful in persuading her to join the Young Conservatives at the

Dove Street Club. At first she was simply attracted by the social events, but was soon involved in campaigning, marking the start of nearly fifty years' involvement in local politics.

Once qualified as a secretary, Eve returned to Norwich, and gained her first job in the office at the recently completed John Mackintosh & Sons chocolate factory, the original having been completely destroyed by a wartime incendiary raid. However, she did not enjoy the experience, and soon left the company to join Anglia Television.

Following her father's funeral in late 1971, Eve faced a momentous decision. She could return to Southern Rhodesia, travel to some other exotic destination, or stay in Norwich. Realising that her mother needed her support, Eve moved back into her old room in Constitution Hill and went job hunting. First she worked at John Oliver's Hairdressers, bookkeeping and juggling diaries for the three partners. Then, tempted by an offer from Air Anglia, she took a job in Fifers Lane, previously RAF Horsham St Faith, from where the tiny airline flew passengers to Amsterdam and Rotterdam on Douglas DC-3 piston engine aircraft. Working for managing directors Jim Crampton and Leslie 'Wilbur' Wright proved challenging. The two men shared an office but were unable to abide each other for very long; as one arrived, the other would leave the room. Jim in particular had a habit of disappearing into the clouds, only to call Eve for help after crash-landing his light aircraft in a farmer's field.

Shoe enthusiast Eve then worked for the managing director of Bally Shoes for about three years, before heading for London to explore the world of public relations and advertising with Chappell Music and Good Relations PR. Finally, frustrated with working for other people, Eve resolved to set up her own business in Norwich, selling designer knitwear. Before starting this venture, Eve embarked on a short trip aboard the Cunard ocean liner *QE2* to New York, returning by the same route to Southampton. With only a few hours of sailing remaining, on 2 April 1982, it was announced that Great Britain was at war with Argentina. The *QE2* was to be commandeered as a troop ship and, following a refit, sent to the South Atlantic to defend the Falkland Islands. The conflict lasted seventy-four days, ending with the Argentine surrender on 14 June.

The following year, Eve opened her franchise 'Event Knitwear', in Bedford Street behind Garlands department store. While Eve travelled the country, mainly to Scotland, buying British-designed garments, her sole staff member ran the shop. The business moved location twice – first to Dove Street and later to Bridewell Alley – before closing in 1993.

On 9 June 1983, the country went to the polls. Eve joined other Conservative Party activists, campaigning in Norwich North, and enjoyed the celebrations when both Norwich North and Norwich South constituencies returned Tory MPs.[3] Military success in the previous year ensured that Margaret Thatcher won the most decisive election victory since that of Labour in 1945. About this time, Eve gave up her knitwear business, bought a house a little further down Constitution Hill and took on a franchise in greetings cards with the Original Poster Company. In 1997, with Mrs Thatcher gone and Tony Blair's Labour Party heading for a massive victory, the Tory County Councillor for Taverham and Drayton retired due to health issues, leaving a vacant seat. Eve was persuaded to stand, and to her relief, was elected.

The year proved challenging: she was still finding her feet at County Hall; lost her two maternal aunts in March and May; and then, most difficult of all, her mother died at the family home in August, aged eighty. All three sisters were gone within five months. It was hardly credible. The pressure on Eve was relentless, working for residents in Taverham and Drayton, as well as arranging probate for four estates. In 1998, she bought Rufus, a Norfolk Terrier cross Bedlington. He would be her closest companion for fifteen years. With his big floppy ears, he became a firm favourite with others enjoying the city parks. In May 2004, Eve stood again for a city seat in Catton Grove Ward, close to Norwich Airport. This time her bid was successful, and she found herself the only Conservative councillor at City Hall. It was a challenging time, with Eve serving on both the county and city councils. In 2006, rookie Conservative Councillor Anthony Little joined her on the 'opposition benches' in City Hall. Three years later, as time approached for the 2009 Lord Mayor nominations, Eve admitted her secret ambition to wear the chain of office. Although tempted to put his own name forward, the much younger Anthony bowed to Eve's greater experience. Eve's nomination was accepted; she would become the 100th Lord Mayor of Norwich, and in time her name was added to the roll of honour outside the Council Chamber.[4]

With no one 'special' in her life, apart from Rufus, when asked to name her official consort, Eve turned to Norwich man Vic Hopes, a close colleague from the Conservative Party. Vic was a widower, much older than Eve, with an eccentric sense of fun. Over the years he had worked in some of the iconic industries most associated with Norwich – beer, shoes and print. He and Eve had met on several occasions, when delivering leaflets or canvassing, or at social events such as the traditional pre-Christmas punch parties held at George Richards' house in Church Lane. It was there in December 2008 that Eve approached Vic with an unusual offer. 'I think I'm likely to be Lord Mayor next year, Vic. I wonder if you might be my consort?' Not believing for one moment that her nomination would be successful, Vic graciously accepted. On arriving home he rang his old friend, Labour Councillor Roy Blower. 'What's this rumour about Eve being put up for Lord Mayor?' Roy laughed. 'It's no rumour, Vic, it's set in stone.' There could be no backing out now.

Not that Vic wanted to change his mind. In fact, having been alone since his wife Kath had died five years earlier, he began to look forward to this unique experience. His only concern was that he knew no one from Norwich 'society'. But Eve knew everyone and soon Vic felt quite at home amongst the inner circle at City Hall, learning to blend in and recognising when to stand back. Eve's Sheriff was environmentalist Tim O'Riordan, a senior academic at the University of East Anglia. The working relationship between him and Eve got off to a delicate start with Tim invariably running late, and he was keen to discuss global warming at any opportunity. Eve, in turn, had a tendency to appear distant, creating barriers until she had eased into her new role. They came from very different worlds.

Eve's civic attendant, chauffeur and sword bearer was former fireman Gavin Thorpe, his knowledge and humour proving priceless. The only problem was Rufus. Gavin was not at all keen to have him inside the Daimler. On arriving at Eve's home to drive her to an engagement, he would often find her out walking the dog. As he sat looking at his watch, she'd turn up, still needing to change into her official robes and eat her habitual bowl of Weetabix. They would then drive to Eaton to collect Vic. The two men always shared a good-natured laugh during those drives, developing a mutual liking and respect for each other, as Eve looked on bemused. Gavin always knew where Eve was in a crowd, her powerful voice rising distinctively above the hubbub. He began to enjoy her company, breaking through her natural reserve and finding a soft core, a glint in her eye and a dry humour. But he still didn't allow Rufus in the car, not even when he was wearing his red coat with the embroidered inscription 'Lord Mayor's Dog'!

Unfortunately, Eve suffered some illness during the very hard winter and was absent from a number of engagements, including the annual King's Lynn Mart, a traditional funfair held in February. Tim was always willing to stand in for her, often at short notice. But she tried not to miss events in support of the civic charity Voluntary Norfolk, and helped raise a sum in excess of £22,000 over the year. There was no shortage of royalty to welcome as First Citizen. The Prince of Wales and the Princess Royal paid the city a visit but the most memorable event was on 4 May 2010, when Her Majesty the Queen and the Duke of Edinburgh came to Norwich, their first official visit in eight years. The Royal couple officially opened the new £12.5 million Hostry and Refectory at Norwich Cathedral, with more than 800 guests filling the pews for the thanksgiving service presided over by Bishop Graham. Eve felt privileged to be seated just across the aisle from the Queen.

Eve was particularly proud to lead the first ever ceremony that saw women being entitled to become a Freeman of Norwich[5], which had been an exclusively male honour for 800 years. On 19 March 2010, Eve and Vic spent the entire evening at St Andrew's Hall, immersed in tradition and ritual, swearing in fifty-four men and 212 women, some of whom had travelled many miles to be there. It was a proud day too for their relatives, coming together to witness the Lord Mayor granting the title Freeman of the City of Norwich to their loved ones. By the end of the night, Eve's smile was beginning to wane from having had to pose for the camera both with the recipient and also with their families.

A lifelong supporter of Norwich City Football Club, Eve was disappointed on 8 May when her team lost 0–2 to Carlisle. Despite this defeat, the Canaries became League One Champions, with Eve leading the celebrations at Norwich Castle. A few days later, with only six days to go until Mayor-Making, the political map of the country radically changed. The general election of 6 May 2010 resulted in none of the parties achieving the 326 votes needed for an overall majority. Eve was delighted to see the end of thirteen years of Labour government, but equally disturbed by the coalition of Conservatives and Liberal Democrats. Just six days after David Cameron became Prime Minister, Eve handed her chain to Green Councillor Tom Dylan, the first member of his party to be so honoured. She then went away on a well-earned holiday, exhausted from attending more than 400 engagements.

Eve continued to represent the residents of Catton Grove for a further twelve months, until losing her seat to Labour Councillor Paul Kendrick. Now there was more time for her to concentrate on renovating a house in North Norfolk, potter in her garden, enjoy music and plan further overseas adventures. Rufus died in 2012, eventually being replaced by a Norfolk terrier called Buster. But Rufus can never be forgotten, as during her mayoral year Eve commissioned a large pastel portrait from Norfolk-based artist Liz Balkwill, showing Eve wearing the red gown and chain of office seated alongside her special friend. The picture still hangs in pride of place in Eve's front room.

Endnotes

1. Southern Rhodesia became Zimbabwe on 18 April 1980.
2. Hilary Arnopp cycled every evening in the blackout to her home in Dereham.
3. Patrick Thompson MP in Norwich North, John Powley MP in Norwich South.
4. Eve stood down from Norfolk County Council when she was made Lord Mayor in 2009.
5. Changes to the Local Democracy, Economic Development and Construction Act 2009, meant that from then on daughters of Freemen could claim the right to that title. The first lady to be so honoured that night was Connie Adam, who in 1990 had begun a campaign against the discrimination, championed by Norman Lamb, MP for North Norfolk.

Evelyn Jean Collishaw 2009–10

Further Highlights from her Mayoral Year

- Seeing the surprised faces of shoppers as a bagpiper led a robed group of civics through the city on her Mayor-Making day.

- As First Citizen, officially welcoming members of the Royal Family to Norwich.

- Shivering in the wind and the hail outside the Forum on May Bank Holiday, alongside the Ambassador of Thailand while costumed Thai ladies valiantly performed a traditional dance display.

- Enjoying superb roast beef and excellent accompanying red wine, as the only female guest at the all-male City Club dinner at Blackfriars Hall.

- Raising upwards of £20,000 for the civic charity Voluntary Norfolk, including playing tenpin bowling in Bowthorpe while wearing the red robes and plumed hat; hosting a fun quiz night complete with pizza supper, and witnessing the first professional valuation of city regalia, including St George's guild sword and the Sheriff's chain, during a charity antiques valuation day at Blackfriars Hall.

- Sharing moments of fun with fellow chain gang members around Norfolk, including fish and chips in Cromer and horse racing in Great Yarmouth.

- Riding in an open-top Mercedes with consort Vic through the streets of Norwich during the 33rd annual Lord Mayor's Procession, with twenty-one walking groups and forty-three floats.

- Welcoming visitors from the French city of Rouen, celebrating the fiftieth anniversary of twinning.

- Having lunch in the Members' Pavilion with the President of the Royal Norfolk Agricultural Association, at the Royal Norfolk Show.

- Opening the first ever Norwich Pride Parade from Chapelfield Gardens, accompanied by the sounds of the Norwich Samba band.

- Celebrating the forthcoming 100th birthday of St John's Roman Catholic Cathedral, to be marked by the completion of the Narthex project, an extension to the Grade I listed building that would provide a community restaurant and learning facilities.

- Opening the Lady Julian Bridge over the Wensum, linking Riverside with the city centre, alongside two nuns, Sister Pamela and Sister Violet, watched over by Rufus the dog.

CHAPTER 14

Jennifer Susan Lay
(1937–2013)
Lord Mayor of Norwich 2011–12

My mum's birth name was Jennifer Susan Pescot. I would like to talk about her character and then talk a little about her struggles with the mystery surrounding her parentage. She was immensely compassionate and protective towards family and friends, passionate about the causes that drove her to enter politics. She was driven and ambitious. She was extremely loyal but despite all that she achieved she lacked confidence in herself and had a deep underlying vulnerability and insecurity. She was extremely modest with high expectations of herself, took risks, encouraged us, my brother and I, to do the same. She was a complex character in many ways, and I believe that links back to her insecurity as a child.

(Susie Lay, speaking in 2016)

Much of Jenny's life was spent as if inside a detective story, searching for clues, interrogating witnesses, and analysing throwaway comments while facing setbacks at every turn. In 1980, Jenny and her husband Ken shared the conundrum with their teenage children, Stephen and Susie. Susie will never forget that day. 'Mum and Dad sat us down and told us this big secret.'[1]

Jenny's mother, Dora Blanche Pescot,[2] from Northchapel in Sussex, became pregnant while working as a single woman at a vicarage in Brighton. While on a weekend break in Northchapel with her sister

Bessie, Dora was driven in a private taxi from her mother's cottage to a nursing hospital away from the village, luxuries her family could never have afforded. Dora gave birth to Jennifer Susan, a month earlier than expected, on 22 August 1937. Jenny's birth certificate has a blank space where the father's name should be. For nearly seven decades, despite rigorous enquiries from her daughter, Dora never disclosed his name, unwilling to betray her sworn oath never to tell.

In 1939, Captain Bruce Bairnsfather,[3] the first British officer cartoonist from the First World War, then fifty-two years old, moved to Northchapel with his wife Ceal, buying a seventeenth-century timber-framed house known as The Old Forge. Very soon after, Dora went to work as housekeeper for the couple. Jenny recalled later how as a child she played on the circular wooden seat surrounding an old tree outside The Forge. This very seat features in a Bairnsfather cartoon in which the artist's well-known character 'Old Bill' is shown nursing a pint of frothing beer, an image which to this day hangs in the Half Moon Pub in Northchapel. Jenny vividly remembered her mother's employer talking gently to her, giving her a sixpence and a doll, which he suggested she call Vivian.[4] As an adult, still contemplating her father's identity, Jenny was perplexed by the enduring secretive attitude of Dora, Bessie and her grandmother Susan Pescot, with whom Jenny had a very special bond. She wondered why each woman steadfastly refused to speak about the celebrated and charismatic village resident. Jenny held on to the fact that her mother had once admitted that she had adored her father.

In 1942, when Jenny was five, Dora married Albert Lionel Churcher.[5] Dora was a feisty and spirited woman, fond of Woodbines and sherry. Lionel was less fond of such indulgences, so Dora settled into a more domestic role. For years, the couple led Jenny to believe that Lionel was her real father. Dora gave birth to Lionel's daughter Ann at the end of 1943. When Jenny was seventeen she overheard an argument between Lionel and Dora, it becoming clear that Lionel was not her natural father. Vulnerable and fragile, the young woman suffered a breakdown, leading to months of treatment. Once recovered, she moved with her parents and sister to Portsmouth, where Jenny joined the Solent Way Nursing Home as a trainee nurse. Once qualified, she transferred to the Portsmouth Infectious Diseases Hospital, where her experiences of caring for adults with polio left a lasting impression on her. During this period Jenny met Kenneth William Lay,[6] one year her senior, who was soon to be demobbed from the Royal Air Force. They married in June 1960 at a traditional white wedding – a love match that would last for fifty-five years.

Despite her newfound happiness, the mystery of Jenny's real father continued to trouble her, and she drew her husband into the intrigue. Being a skilled cartoonist himself, Ken was fascinated by the fact that Dora had worked for Bruce Bairnsfather and began buying his drawings, photographs, books and other memorabilia. He would deliberately display them on the dining table when Dora came to visit, hoping to inveigle her into talking about her time with him. But strangely, she ignored them.

Jenny and Ken had two children, Stephen born in March 1962, and Susan in July 1966. Ken enrolled at college, his ambition a career in the Home Office, initially as an assistant prison governor. Success meant his family living in various locations, including Feltham, Birmingham and Spixworth in Norfolk. They certainly met some characters along the way. In Feltham, Jenny was delighted when a young offender transformed her garden into a colourful oasis of blooms, only to discover later that he had transplanted them from the governor's garden.

With his children aged twelve and eight, Ken took a posting at HMP Norwich, the family renting a house in Spixworth. Susie loved her time at Woodland View School, and was sorry to leave three years later when transferring to Birmingham. It was here that Susie first became aware of her mother's burgeoning interest in local politics:

> People from the Conservative Party kept coming round for meetings. I opened the door to them and tried to be polite, but spent most of the time hiding upstairs. There were boxes of leaflets everywhere. Even the word leaflet now fills me with horror.[7]

Jenny was now desperate to settle down in one place and anxious that her children should establish roots. But the prison service preferred its staff to remain flexible, available for short-notice postings. Jenny and Ken bought a weekend home in Spixworth, an interim measure while Ken applied for a move to Norwich Prison, specifically requesting a long-term contract. Delighted when the authorities proved amenable, the family moved into Mons Avenue on Mousehold Heath in Norwich in 1978. Their house, just a short walk from the prison, was a large ramshackle property full of period features, mysterious spaces and an extensive garden in need of much attention. It was positioned on an area of heathland and woodland, with exceptional views across the city to the horizon beyond, in an area designated as a nature reserve. Jenny loved it. Once Ken was permitted to purchase the house, Jenny knew this would be their 'forever' family home. Working in the Artificial Limbs and Appliances Centre in Exchange Street, she dealt mainly with applications for wheelchairs. After that she spent eight years working as a residential social worker, retiring in 1996 as night manager in homes for the elderly.

In 1984, Susie completed the foundation year at Norwich School of Art, followed by an Honours Degree in Fine Art in 1989. Politically, Jenny withdrew from the Conservatives, for a short time toying with the recently established Social Democrat Party before joining the Labour Party in 1990. She was soon persuaded to become secretary of her branch and her name regularly appeared on ballot papers. Mons Avenue became a meeting place for local party activists. As well as her strong Christian faith, Jenny held a passionate belief that all living creatures were sacred, be they dogs, cats, insects, plants or garden birds – a doctrine she passed on to her children. But despite this, Jenny was not fond of the outdoors, with Susie being assigned to walk the family dogs, many of which were adopted from rescue centres.

In May 1996, Jenny was elected to Mancroft Ward, her first seat as a city councillor. Only two years later, she was nominated as Sheriff of Norwich, working with Liberal Democrat Lord Mayor Derek Wood, and she quickly became immersed in her civic duties. She was involved with the formation of the Norwich Sheriff's Association, and worked closely with Councillor Doug Underwood, who in 2007 became the first Chairman of the Norwich Civic Association.[8] The twelve months proved rewarding but challenging, with Jenny and Derek approaching their roles very differently, and unfortunately creating some tensions between Lord Mayor and the Sheriff's husband. Despite this, Ken remained a constant support to his wife. He later committed his thoughts to paper in one of his legendary comic poems. Entitled *The Sheriff's Consort*, it closed on a prophetic note:

Be considerate to the consort

He lives in a world of his own.

He is not fêted, robed or chained,

In fact he is hardly ever known.

He never complains, why should he?

He didn't earn his place in the sun.

He bathes in reflected glory

Of just about everyone.

So be considerate to the consort

He wasn't born to be less

And then one day if the cards go his way

They'll make him the Lady Mayoress.[9]

Early in 2000, Jenny put her name forward as Lord Mayor for the Millennium year. She was up against keen birdwatcher and former post office manager Ron Borett. Jenny lost the vote and it was Ron who had the pleasure of presenting American playwright Arthur Miller with the honorary Freedom of the City. Her disappointment was exacerbated when she lost her council seat at the May elections. However, for the following four years, Jenny continued to work tirelessly with community organisations and schools, as well as with the Labour Party. Successfully returned to City Hall in 2004 with a seat in Crome Ward, over the subsequent four years Jenny showed signs of strain. Her family was worried. Susie, now working for Norfolk Wildlife Trust, was concerned to hear that her mother was consulting a doctor:

> Mum told me about the lump in her breast and asked me to go with her to the specialist. They talked about operating. Mum was stoic but to be honest I was in shock. She was devastated at the thought of a double mastectomy. Sadly, at the same time our elderly chocolate Labrador Bourneville had to be put to sleep. It was a challenging, difficult and desperately sad time.[10]

Jenny's surgery and a course of radiotherapy appeared to eradicate her cancer, and within six months she was once again fully immersed in her council work. Late in 2010, council leaders debated whether Councillor Lay was now well enough to be considered as Lord Mayor for 2011–12. The answer was a resounding 'yes', providing a long-awaited champagne moment for the family. With the City Council actively seeking closer relationships between the public and civic leaders, Councillor Keith Driver[11] had no hesitation in nominating local publican Chris Higgins as Sheriff, the first landlord to be so honoured. The Trafford Arms in Town Close was a popular watering hole for council staff, councillors and former civics, and the landlord was an enthusiastic fundraiser for local charities. Chris and his wife Glynis, both with little experience of local politics, were understandably nervous. Jenny immediately put them at ease. Chris was discreetly made aware of Jenny's past illness and was asked to stand in for her at short notice should she become unwell. As their civic charity, out of respect and gratitude for her care, Jenny nominated the Big C Cancer Support and Information Centre at the Norfolk and Norwich Hospital.

The civic year began well with the annual Civic Service, visits to a swimming gala and a fashion show, greeting cyclists at City Hall, opening Refugee Week and presenting prizes at Norwich School Speech Day. But by the opening day of the Norfolk Royal Show in early July, Jenny had suffered a relapse. With only an hour to go before the President's Luncheon, Chris received a call at the pub. Civic Attendant Gavin Thorpe would drive them to the showground in fifteen minutes. Glynis was summoned from her shopping, and both were dressed appropriately by the time Gavin arrived. Later that summer, Chris and Glynis made a last-minute dash to Buckingham Palace, Jenny being devastated at missing her opportunity to walk on the hallowed lawns. She did, however, attend a smaller, more intimate affair at Sandringham later in the year. For the majority of the year the civic party worked together, Jenny's gentle sympathetic approach complementing Chris's ebullient warmth. Jenny and Glynis became good friends, enjoying a glass of wine over countless buffet tables. Chris, Glynis and Gavin all enjoyed Ken's dry humour, discovering his love of amateur acting. After a time, much to everyone's distress, it became increasingly apparent that Ken was showing early signs of dementia. Gavin would often find him sitting in front of the television, unaware that he was expected at a function. Ken tired quickly, and found excuses to leave early from engagements. Despite this, all four of the civic party looked forward to developing their friendship once this special year was over.

By mid-July, Jenny was well enough to attend her Lord Mayor's Procession, heading up the parade, despite the weight of the robe and chain sitting heavily on her tiny frame. She walked the entire route alongside Ken and her civic team, and was thrilled when £5,500 was raised for the Big C charity. By the end of her mayoral year, the total had risen to over £25,000. Everyone loved Jenny. Letters regularly appeared in the local press from residents, charities and businesses, thanking her for being such an inspirational civic leader. At the annual dinner of the Norwich Civic Association, speaking to an audience of former Lord Mayors and Sheriffs, she paid tribute to her husband:

> Ken has been my stay and support for fifty-two years. We have been through some tough times, some anxious ones and some hilariously funny ones. I would never have had the confidence to

be Lord Mayor of Norwich if it had not been for his support and encouragement.

Jenny had loved being a councillor, Sheriff and Lord Mayor, each role suiting her many strengths. She had genuine affection, rapport and empathy for people, but at seventy-five, with her stamina draining away, enough was enough. She did not stand for election again, and asked her friend Councillor Marion Maxwell to consider standing for her seat.[12]

During the summer of 2012, Susie received a call from her brother. Could she come to the house straightaway? Jenny had the worst possible news. The situation at home worsened when, two months later, Ken suffered a sudden stroke. He was taken to hospital but discharged himself four days later, refusing to be separated from Jenny. His physical recovery was remarkably rapid, but as Jenny's condition deteriorated, Ken became increasingly confused. Susie moved in with her parents, facing an unprecedented uphill struggle. Wishing to shield her daughter from further upset, Jenny secretly took Stephen and close friend Council Leader Alan Waters to discuss funeral arrangements with her vicar, the Reverend Christopher Ellis. Collectively, they chose the music, readings and hymns. Stephen's professional experience as a mentor to student nurses helped him face this most difficult of discussions. Soon there was no choice but to admit Jenny to the Norfolk and Norwich Hospital for palliative care. Although desperately concerned about Ken, she was confident that her children would take good care of him. During her final week, Ken was too distressed to visit his wife. Understanding him as she did, Jenny did not complain, instead taking comfort from his photograph. On the afternoon of 12 July 2013, as Gavin prepared to visit the hospital, he received a call from Chris Higgins breaking the news that Jenny had died earlier that day.

The church was overflowing. Stephen, Alan Waters and Chris Higgins had prepared personal tributes, evoking memories and tears amongst the mourners. The only person missing was Ken. Stephen recalls the heartbreaking decision that Ken made, and which, out of love and respect for their father, they had to accept:

> On the morning of the service, Susie and I encouraged him to come with us but he was very tearful and he felt that he was simply not up to it. Instead he wrote a short and beautiful eulogy about how he and Mum had promised to stay together and how in death as in life, they would always be together.[13]

As his children left the house, Ken double-checked the estimated finishing time. At 11.45 am, directly following the commendation, the exit music sounded up. The familiar tune of *Feed the Birds*, from Disney's *Mary Poppins*, filled the church. It was simple, classic and touching: a reminder of Jenny's love of all things in the natural world. At that very moment in Mons Avenue, Ken lifted a 12 kilogram bag of birdseed, liberally scattering the contents in between plants, over paths and under hedges, until it drifted like snow and crunched beneath his feet.

A year later, almost to the day that Jenny died, Ken became seriously ill. He never fully regained his strength, at times uncertain about where Jenny might be. But throughout, he retained his sense of humour, bringing a modicum of consolation to his children. Ken died on 25 July 2014, aged seventy-seven. The family decided a traditional funeral would not be appropriate. Instead, a tape recording was played at the crematorium, Ken's familiar voice filling the space as he told stories, sang comic songs and recited from Shakespeare – recordings he had made for fun decades earlier, never suspecting that their first public outing would be at his own funeral. To complement this, Susie designed the order of service to resemble a theatre programme, complete with cast list and photographs. Both Ken and Jenny would have enjoyed the joke.

And what of Bruce Bairnsfather? While visiting Dora in a Portsmouth Nursing home in 2006, Jenny and Ken had grasped their final opportunity to resolve the puzzle. Bringing the conversation around to memories of the The Old Forge, Jenny asked her mother: 'Was Bruce Bairnsfather my father?' Dora responded firmly: 'I don't think we should talk about this anymore.' In December 2011, Susie and Stephen, independently and without telling each other, wrote to writer and biographer Mark Warby, who was responsible in 1999 for resurrecting the *Old Bill Newsletter*, a publication for fans of Bairnsfather's work.[14] For three months, Susie and Mark exchanged emails and shared information. But with the passing of time, evidence remained circumstantial, with no new findings coming to light. Susie was disappointed but remains skeptical:

> We would all like to think we were related to someone who had such prestige and talent, so well known. I would love it to be him because my mum always felt it was. My dad was convinced too, but without hard evidence we have not allowed ourselves to hope. Instead we treasure the cartoon of 'Old Bill' that Bairnsfather drew

for Dora in his sketchbook in his studio at The Old Forge, a gift for her shortly before she married Lionel.[15]

Stephen and Susie may never discover the identity of their mother's father. But they are deeply proud to be the son and daughter of a woman who, despite being a reluctant cook, made sure her family never went hungry; who, if a spider dropped into the dog's water bowl, came to the rescue with a piece of tissue paper; who wore pink ankle boots under her civic gown; who selflessly worried that her children were having to deal with their parents' illnesses; who was never too busy to empathise with a troubled soul, always ready with a smile and a reassuring touch on the arm; and who was respected and admired by colleagues of all political hues, an exemplary councillor and a popular and much loved Lord Mayor.

Endnotes

1. Susie Lay, talking in 2016.
2. Dora Blanche Pescot, 1911–2006.
3. Charles Bruce Bairnsfather, 1887–1959.
4. Vivian Carter was a lifelong friend of Bairnsfather and editor of *The Bystander* magazine, since 1915 regularly publishing work by the artist.
5. Albert Lionel Churcher, 1898–1964. He was medically discharged from the Royal Sussex Regiment in March 1919, having served as a gunner at the front, injured in action.
6. Kenneth William Lay, 1936–2014.
7. Susie Lay, talking in 2016.
8. The City of Norwich Civic Association was established in 2007 by former Lord Mayor Michael Banham, who said that while there was an organisation for Sheriffs locally and nationally, there was nothing for Lord Mayors. Its aim is to promote, preserve and enhance the tradition of the civic offices, to represent Norwich and promote the city. Membership is open to former Lord Mayors, former Sheriffs, partners and consorts. They hold meetings and dinners throughout the year, as well as meeting at civic events.
9. Unpublished poem written by Kenneth Lay in 1998.
10. Susie Lay, speaking in 2016.
11. Keith Driver was Lord Mayor 2013–14.
12. Marion Maxwell was Lord Mayor 2016–17.
13. Stephen Lay, writing in 2017.
14. http://www.brucebairnsfather.org.uk
15. Susie Lay, writing in 2017.

Jennifer Susan Lay 2011-12

Further Highlights from her Mayoral Year

- Switching on the Christmas tree lights at the Marie Curie Cancer Care service at Norwich Cathedral.

- Being enchanted at County Hall by the East Coast Truckers and waving off the annual convoy of local disadvantaged children, horns sounding, on their way to a day out at Pleasurewood Hills.

- Receiving an unexpected gift from Len Mann, a veteran of Normandy at the D-Day Remembrance Service. He presented Jenny with a badge commemorating the Normandy campaign, with the date 1944–2011.

- Witnessing Richard Jewson plant a new rose, named 'Friend of Strangers', in the garden of Strangers' Hall to celebrate the ninetieth anniversary of the museum.

- Attending the Norwich Sports Awards at City Hall, hearing inspirational stories from young people, who despite suffering from disability and illness, achieved success in a variety of sports over the year.

- Attending the AGM of the Magdalen Group, an organisation opened in 1992 dedicated to supporting and helping sex workers in the city and hearing about the success of its outreach teams.

- Raising a total of £5,568.99 at the Lord Mayor's Celebrations for the civic charity Big C, far higher than the projected £4,000.

- Presenting certificates to thirty-four newly created Freemen of the City of Norwich, including Charley and Pam South, landlords of the Brickmakers Pub – a popular live music pub on the Sprowston Road.

- Being the first to greet Charles, the Prince of Wales, to the Priscilla Bacon Centre during his visit to Norfolk. Talking with the nurses, office staff and chaplain before the Royal car swept into the car park, escorted by police motorcycles, all lights blazing.

- Arriving at Norwich Cathedral at 6.45 am to start a charity bike race including more than 1,000 bicycles, in aid of the British Heart Foundation.

- Helping to celebrate the sixtieth wedding anniversary of Len and Beryl Watkins, parents of Brian Watkins, who was Sheriff of Norwich in 1990.

- Joining former England cricketer Sir Ian Botham outside City Hall as he set off on a sponsored 'Beefy Walk', raising money for children suffering from leukaemia.

CHAPTER 15

Judith Elizabeth Lubbock (1952–)

Lord Mayor of Norwich 2014–15

The cycle campaign wanted VIPs to promote cycling. I was very keen as I am a cyclist. But of course there were limitations as Lord Mayor. You can't cycle to events in robes and chains! When I went for a health check at a local chemist I arrived on my bike and I cycled to the celebration of Dr Bike's Cycling Workshop at the UEA. I simply wore my Lord Mayor's badge on the ribbon. I didn't really want Gavin driving along in a car with my bits and pieces, as this would have undermined the environmental and health message I was trying to give.

(Judith Lubbock, speaking in 2016)

Like all fathers, former Royal Naval Signaller Edwin Herbert Barrow[1] wanted to provide the best life possible for his wife, Doris Lilian,[2] and three daughters, Sharon, Judith and Katherine. He joined the Royal Navy in 1932, training as a specialist in military communications, transmitting, receiving, encoding, decoding and distributing messages on minesweepers and aircraft carriers throughout the war. Eddie's 25-year career necessitated countless disruptive house moves including to Lossiemouth and Portsmouth, and periods lodging with the in-laws. But once Sharon was born in 1950, there was a need for a more permanent home: a two-bedroomed council flat in Hanworth, Middlesex. Shortly afterwards, Eddie left the 'Senior Service', with his Long Service and

Good Conduct medals, finding his qualifications to be exactly those that Post Office Telecommunications were looking for.

The world of communications was advancing at a rapid rate and Eddie was well placed to play a significant part in its development. He made the long commute to Victoria Embankment to the headquarters of Cable & Wireless, while Dora took a job locally as a typist. They both worked long hours to ensure their family was well provided for, and were soon able to upgrade to a new three-bedroomed second-floor flat in the suburb of Hampton, on the north bank of the river Thames. The family had never before owned a telephone, always using the red telephone boxes. The girls were thrilled with their first party line, which frequently meant briefly overhearing neighbours' conversations before asking, 'When will they get off our phone?' Their home in Hampton must have seemed a paradise, being well positioned for excursions and exploration. Hampton Court Palace, Bushy and Richmond parks offered a thousand acres of grasslands on their doorstep, and with Hampton Ferry and the open-air lido, there was never a reason to be bored. Judith recalls a happy childhood, being cared for by loving parents who saved hard all year to take the girls on camping holidays to Switzerland and Germany, five up in a Ford Anglia with a budget of £100 for the fortnight.

Born on 19 April 1952, Judith passed the 11-plus exam, her proud parents enrolling her at Thames Valley Grammar School, an 'unconventional co-educational grammar school'[3] dating from 1928. When her sixth form timetable for 'A' levels in English and Geography left a little spare time, Judith came up with an initiative that would ultimately prove a formative experience. She and two school friends volunteered at the Normansfield Hospital[4] in Teddington, a residential institution for people with mental health issues and learning difficulties. For the young ladies from Thames Valley Grammar it was a grim and daunting place, seemingly unchanged from the Victorian asylum it once was, the huge grey exterior concealing Spartan conditions, unsavoury smells and frustrated staff. One teenage resident was Shelley Rix, born with Down's syndrome, the daughter of well-known comedy actor and mental health campaigner Brian Rix. Shocked and humbled, for two years the friends kept returning, diligently carrying out basic tasks, including spoon-feeding patients and learning the art of compassion and tolerance in the face of those who are 'different'. For this, Judith was awarded a school prize for service to the community.

With an ambition to teach she chose to study Early Years Learning at the Redland Teacher Training College in Bristol. It was during one of the many student parties that Judith met Nigel Lubbock,[5] a law student at Bristol University. During their courtship, Judith heard stories of Nigel's birthplace and home until the age of ten – the distant city of Norwich in darkest East Anglia. When HM Prison Service promoted his prison officer father to Brixton, the Lubbock family left Norwich for London. Judith and Nigel were married in Hampton on 21 July 1973. Judith was twenty-one. Nigel, hankering after his childhood haunts, had already a position as an articled clerk at Howard Killin & Bruce, a Norwich law firm. But Judith was still unemployed. They honeymooned in Norwich, a pragmatic decision as Judith had secured a job interview at Norwich City Council, at that time the authority responsible for education in the city. She was immediately offered a teaching post at Ranworth Road Primary School. Although delighted, Judith admitted that she and her new husband had nowhere yet to live. The officer suggested a one-year service tenancy agreement, after which period they would have to vacate. Consequently, an affordable one-bedroomed flat in Mile Cross became their first married home, from where Nigel could walk to the office in Prince of Wales Road and Judith caught the bus around the ring road to the Larkman estate.

It was tough settling in. Straight out of college, Judith was simultaneously learning how to be a wife and a teacher, in a city she didn't know, and separated from her parents, with very little money and few friends. Her sanity was saved by the developing friendship with neighbours Anne and Harry, each couple hosting supper parties or sharing a round of drinks in the pub. Following their son's example, Nigel's parents, Clifford and Olive, had moved from London to Acle, a village east of Norwich, routinely inviting Nigel and his young wife to join them for a Sunday roast. During that first year, Judith and Nigel saved enough money to place a deposit on a new build bungalow in Taverham, as well as to buy a small car – a necessity once Nigel relocated to Gervais Steele Solicitors, the offices being 20 miles away in the South Norfolk town of Harleston. Although the travelling was onerous, Nigel's career in the law was on the up.

By contrast, Judith was suffering a crisis; she felt isolated and frustrated at work, reluctantly concluding that teaching was not, after all, for her. After two years of selling advertising space at the *Eastern Daily Press* in Rouen House, Judith began working in the Unemployment Benefit Office in Colegate, the job proving a revelation as she witnessed at first hand the desperation of the unemployed, single mothers, people with disabilities and those in debt, each a hostage to the vagaries of the benefits system. Emotions often ran high, with Judith and her colleagues grateful for the protective counter between them and the clients.

Over the following decade Judith became very familiar with wooden packing crates as Nigel's ambition translated into a series of house moves, some more profitable than others, while balancing the convenience of proximity to the city with the commuting distance from work. In 1982, while living in Harleston, their first child Tom was born. Judith had wanted a baby for some time, but Nigel needed some persuasion that the time was right. Despite his previous reticence, Nigel fell instantly in love with their child. It was time for another house move, Nigel being tempted by a barn ripe for conversion in the nearby village of Starston. Builders took over the barn, promising original beams and a spacious mezzanine level, while the Lubbocks camped out in a tiny cottage, where daughter Ana was born in 1984. The finished barn was perfect for a growing family.[6]

One morning, the doorbell rang. If Judith had not been at home that day, her future could have been very different. She listened politely to the Liberal Democrat canvasser, empathising with his views and inviting him in so she could hear more. It wasn't long before she was co-opted onto the fundraising committee for South Norfolk Liberal Democrats, and she volunteered to hold a party at the barn. More events followed, Judith establishing friendships with like-minded people who would feature in her life for many decades to come. Nigel was bemused by his wife's new interest, and supported her by babysitting when required. He was aware of the party; a colleague at work was former employment solicitor and City Councillor Norman Lamb[7], who had joined Steeles Law in 1987. This charismatic politician would be an inspiration for Judith when considering her own future in local politics.

Still not yet ready to settle, Nigel continued to initiate a further series of house purchases and investments, including a weekend bolt-hole in Walberswick on the Suffolk coast. Finally, in 1990, two years after the death of Judith's father, and the children now aged eight and six, they bought their 'forever' home at the far end of Unthank Road: an impressive Edwardian detached home with an extensive garden, where they live to this day. With inevitable bills to pay, Judith returned to teaching, taking a post at West Earlham First School. It was a tough school, tempered by a supportive, caring ethos. Judith loved the job. She joined the Liberal Democrats in Norwich South, helping with the campaign to elect local accountant Ian Couzens as a city councillor for Eaton, Judith's new home territory. At the second attempt in 1994, the party was successful, taking a seat from the Conservatives. Twelve months later, Judith was persuaded to join Ian on the ballot paper, and was astonished when she won by 300 votes. Her party was on a roll, and in 1996, the third and final City Council seat also fell to a Liberal Democrat. Eaton had a full house.

From the very start she adopted a professional attitude, responding to all comers, however trivial their request might seem. If she couldn't deal with someone's issue, she was sure to direct them to someone who could. She studied every piece of paper that arrived from City Hall, dissecting agendas in advance of meetings, double-checking facts, preparing responses and drafting speeches. Over her sixteen years on the Planning Committee, Judith became renowned for her knowledge of planning law, conscientious research and powers of persuasion when promoting her arguments.

To date, Judith has been re-elected four times, regularly exasperating the local Conservative Party who, like many others, considers this affluent middle-class suburb to be natural Tory territory. Despite her busy schedule, she always made time for her ailing mother, who eventually died in a Norwich nursing home in 2013. With her mother gone, and Nigel able to work part-time hours, Judith approached James Wright, Leader of the Liberal Democrat group, letting it be known that for her the time was now right and she was willing to be nominated as Lord Mayor. With European Elections scheduled for May, Judith had to wait until 10 June for her proudest moment. The day was set fair, family members were gathered at the house and Nigel was 'suited and booted'. Civic Attendant Gavin Thorpe arrived in good time to drive them the short distance to City Hall.

When offered the choice by City Hall, Judith picked out the most flamboyant of the various mayoral hats, featuring the largest black ostrich feathers. The traditional robes suited her natural elegance, Gavin later admitting, 'She would put on her black and gold robes and big fluffy hat and I always thought she was the most glamorous lady I had looked after.' On 10 June 2014, Judith became the fifteenth female Lord Mayor of Norwich. She opened her acceptance speech by referring to both Ethel Colman and Dorothy Jewson, citing the success of these great ladies as an 'indication of how forward-thinking the citizens of Norwich were', and concluding with a rash promise: 'I would like, as my final event next year, to welcome the Norwich City Football Club, to celebrate their promotion back to the Premier League.[8] Or is that just wishful thinking?' Sharing Judith's limelight on Mayor-Making day was the new Sheriff of Norwich, former City Coroner and Chairman of Cruse Bereavement Care, William Armstrong. Modest, accomplished, highly intelligent and a devout Christian, standing tall in his purple robes and 'Pugwash' hat, he was quietly delighted with the choice of Cruse as the civic charity for the year. The 2014–15 civic team was ready for action.

Judith publicly announced her three aims for the civic year, determined to lead by example. Firstly she would encourage walking and cycling as a pathway to better health, demonstrating this in June when joining VIP Bike Ride alongside other invited city councillors and the City Council Cycling Officer, as they toured both recent and future developments for city cyclists. Judith – ever the consummate host – provided tea and homemade cakes at the end of the route. On another occasion, she arrived by bicycle at the launch of a new Cycle Republic store in Castle Mall, and the press were rewarded with a rare photo opportunity of a Lord Mayor in a cycle helmet. She impressed the Norfolk Sea Scouts by joining them on the Wensum, happy to board a canoe alongside the youngsters. The same mode of transport featured on 26 November, when under miserable skies, having been warned to wear appropriate clothing, Judith stood on the riverbank at the new canoe launch point in Carey's Meadow in Thorpe Road. The official group included the Chairman of Broadland District Council, who preferred to keep his feet dry. Gavin was also more than happy to observe from the bank, his duty being to look after the gold chain. But this engagement was a welcome adventure for Judith, her wide smile betraying her enjoyment, as she confidently paddled the bright red canoe towards the city, accompanied by experienced canoeist John Packman, CEO of the Broads Authority.

Judith's second aim was to celebrate and promote the parks of Norwich as places of relaxation and exercise, showing the way by walking around seven such spaces, including all four of the city's historic parks – Eaton, Heigham, Wensum and Waterloo. Despite her packed civic schedule, whenever possible Judith observed her regular Friday morning practice of walking the short distance from her home to Eaton Park. This had been built during the 1920s, with model boating lake, lily ponds, pavilions, leisure areas and more than forty tennis courts. As a new councillor for Eaton, Judith had responded to complaints about anti-social behaviour in the park by setting up Friends of Eaton Park, an initiative since replicated in a number of the other parks in the city. Members fundraise to improve the amenities and on Friday mornings meet to 'Walk Around the Park', monitoring vandalism or maintenance issues, followed by coffee and cake at the Pavilion Café.

As Chair of the Norwich Preservation Trust, Judith was well placed to promote her third aim: to celebrate the city's history through its great buildings. During Heritage Open Days she volunteered as a steward, ushering people into their seats during events held at the fifteenth-century Guildhall. Confusion arose when Judith spent a day working with the team of volunteers known as City Hosts, wearing the distinctive blue vest emblazoned with the slogan 'Here to Help'. One elderly couple, dubious about her identity, insisted on being photographed alongside this 'so-called' Lord Mayor in order later to verify her unlikely claim!

With her usual attention to detail and careful preparation, Judith embraced the solemnity and tradition of the city's annual civic events. But she was also determined to have fun by: hosting a black-tie civic charity ball at Carrow Road with roulette wheels and blackjack tables, overlooking the football pitch; being seen 'getting down with the kids' at Earlham Park for the Big Weekend hosted by BBC Radio 1; and kicking up her heels on the Forum steps, as she danced alongside freelance journalist Rick Jones who, dressed as Elizabethan actor Will Kemp – complete with jester hat, Morris dancing handkerchiefs and lute – was concluding his challenging recreation of the famous 'Nine Days' Wonder', when Kemp danced the 108 miles from London to Norwich in 1600.

Judith received many invitations as Lord Mayor, two in particular proving particularly memorable. On 28 July 2014, the country commemorated the centenary of the start of the First World War. To mark the occasion, Judith and Nigel were invited to the Tower of London by Norfolk resident and Constable of the Tower, General the Lord Richard Dannatt and his wife Lady Pippa Dannatt. Along with seven other members of the Norfolk Chain Gang, the Chief Constable and the Chief Fire Officer, they began the evening by walking amongst the sea of ceramic poppies installed in the moat, an art installation to be progressively expanded by 11 November into an ocean of 888,246 blood red blooms – one for each British and Commonwealth soldier who died during the conflict. As the sun set, the Norfolk group listened, heads bowed, as the names of those who had died on that date, 100 years earlier, were read aloud. This ritual was carried out every night for four months. The group then viewed the Crown Jewels, without having to queue behind the usual long line of tourists. The doors to the Jewel House opened and then ominously shut behind them. After dinner, Lord Dannatt performed the 700-year-old ritual known as the Ceremony of the Keys, as the Tower was locked for the night.

In February 2015, Judith and Nigel were guests at the annual Celebration of the Day of the City in Novi Sad, the second largest city in Serbia, twinned with Norwich since 1985.[9] Guiding them through the protocol were Peter and Diana Beckley, originators of the Norfolk and Norwich Novi Sad Association. Diana outlined how, in March 1999, NATO bombing raids on the then Yugoslavia destroyed the three bridges over the Danube, effectively marooning the population. Immediately, volunteers from Norwich, including Peter and Diana, raised money and collected foodstuffs, clothing and medical supplies, and drove across Europe to deliver aid to the city. Each year, on arrival at the sumptuous celebration meal, representatives from Norwich are the first to be welcomed – a mark of respect for the city, which is still held in high regard. Judith flew home from Belgrade with a heightened sense of the importance of twinning, resolving to campaign for an increased twinning budget, thus enabling Norwich to reciprocate the generous hospitality routinely shown by its twinned cities.

So what about Judith's dream to welcome Norwich City Football Team, as Lord Mayor, back to the Premier Division? Confidence was high throughout the 2014–15 season. On 26 December, the team gave the fans a late Christmas present with a 6–1 home win against Millwall. Norwich won the emotionally charged local derby against Ipswich Town, ultimately reaching the Championship Play-off against Middlesbrough at Wembley on 25 May 2015, just twenty-four hours before her term as Lord Mayor of Norwich came to an end. Judith and Nigel, son Tom and his wife Nicola (her first football match) joined 40,000 excited Norwich City fans at the iconic stadium, which was awash with yellow and green. And the result? A resounding 2–0 win, guaranteeing Norwich City promotion to the Premier League, and coming not a moment too soon for Judith to claim it as her own.

Endnotes

1. Edwin Herbert Barrow was born in Fulham, West London, on 21 July 1916, the son of a London taxi driver. During the Second World War, Eddie (as he preferred to be known) saw active service on aircraft carriers.
2. Doris Lilian Allen was born in Islington in 1924, one of thirteen, including half-siblings. Both her parents were profoundly deaf. Consequently, the older children took on added responsibilities. Doris did well at school,

working as a typist in Somerset House in London. During the Second World War she joined the Women's Royal Naval Service, where she met Edwin.

3. http://www.twickenham-museum.org.uk/

4. http://ezitis.myzen.co.uk/normansfield.html

5. Nigel is a distant relative of Liberal MP and human rights campaigner, the late Eric Lubbock (Lord Avebury), who won an unexpected by-election in Orpington, Kent, in 1962, decisively overturning the Conservative majority of over 14,000.

6. During the Great Storm of October 1987, Judith and Nigel watched transfixed as the glass shifted from side to side in the double height windows and all the tiles from one side of the roof blew away in the gale.

7. Norman Lamb was elected as MP for North Norfolk in 1992, following ten years of failed attempts. As part of the coalition government of 2010, Norman held various cabinet posts, including Minister of State for Health in 2012.

8. Norwich Football Club had been relegated to the Championship in May 2014.

9. The Novi Sad Friendship Bridge over the river Wensum in Norwich was opened in November 2001.

Lord Mayor Judith Elizabeth Lubbock 2014–15

Further Highlightls From Her Mayoral Year

- Witnessing the installation of the Very Reverend Dr Jane Hodges, the first female dean in the 900-year history of Norwich Cathedral, amongst a congregation of nearly 1,000.

- Hosting twenty-three tea parties in the Lord Mayor's Parlour, serving homemade lemon drizzle cake, brownies and cheese flapjacks.

- Raising in excess of £24,000 for the civic charity Cruse Bereavement Care in Norwich.

- Donning a blue 'Here to Help' City Host tabard and spending a day experiencing the work of the volunteers – part of the Norwich Business Improvement District.

- Walking the Norwich parks to encourage the formation of 'Friends of the Park' groups.

- Enjoying the wonderful music of Serbian pianist Aleksandar Djermanovic at the annual Paul Cross Memorial Concert at the Assembly House. (Paul was the former Chairman of the Norfolk and Norwich Novi Sad Association.)

- Contributing to a historical initiative at the invitation of the Abraham Lincoln Presidential Library and Museum in Springfield, Illinois, to commemorate the 150th anniversary of the assassination of Abraham Lincoln.

- Joining the Norwich City Fans at Wembley, all dressed in yellow and green, to witness the historic Sky Bet Championship Play-Off Final against Middlesbrough, when a 2–0 win meant the Canaries finished the season top of the League with promotion to the Premier League.

- Playing at being a disc jockey during a Radio 1 promotional event at Open on Bank Plain with BBC DJ Greg James.

- Joining the Norwich Whifflers and Snap the Dragon at the Lord Mayor's Procession and watching the firework display from Norwich Castle.

- Celebrating the 75th anniversary of the opening of City Hall.

- Spinning on a roundabout in the playground with pupils of the Clare Special School.

- Turning in circles when playing wheelchair basketball at UEA Sportspark with the Lowriders, members of British Wheelchair Basketball.

CHAPTER 16

Brenda Arthur
(1947–)
Lord Mayor of Norwich 2015–16

Brenda wanted the best for everybody. She became emotional giving talks and speeches because she was so passionate about Norwich. She was invited to be a guest speaker at the City College graduation ceremony at the cathedral. No Lord Mayor or Sheriff had ever been asked before. She was fantastic. She always worried about speeches but every speech she made was a success. And the students cheered her. Sometimes she came across as not being confident, but she was actually very capable and experienced.

(Gavin Thorpe, Civic Attendant, speaking in 2017)

The photograph published in the *Eastern Daily Press* on 22 June 2015 showed four women standing together outside Norwich Cathedral, each wearing their own particular traditional robes. The headline read 'A celebration of women in society'; the occasion was the annual Civic Service. For the first time in 900 years of the city's history, women simultaneously held four of the top civic and theological roles: Dean, Archdeacon, Lord Mayor and Sheriff. Only a month earlier, in the Council Chamber of Norwich City Council, Lord Mayor Brenda Arthur swapped power for pomp. Her election to City Council in 2008 had marked the beginning of an extraordinary and accelerated career in local politics.

This must have seemed a long way from her early days in Birmingham, at Holly Lodge Grammar School and determining the sex of fruit flies. Described by the midwife as a stubborn baby, Brenda was born on 5 April 1947, the only child of Ernest and Irene Hird.[1] During the Second World War, Ernest had served in the Royal Navy, and was involved in the rescue from the Atlantic of evacuated children, their ship bombed by the Germans en route to safety in Canada. When the war was over, Ernest began work as a chargehand on the factory floor at cycle giants Phillips, switching to rivals Raleigh in 1957. Irene, a trained hairdresser, had contracted rheumatic chorea[2] at eleven, leaving her prone to epileptic fits.

Ernest and Irene brought up their daughter in a traditional Victorian terrace working-class home, both believing in tolerance and acceptance at a time when Smethwick – with the second highest immigrant population in the country – was thought to be the most racist town in Britain. From the late 1950s, thousands of Sikh men, dubbed the 'Sikhs of Smethwick', left the impoverished Punjab, seeking work in the steel factories of Britain's Black Country.[3] In 1964, the Conservative MP Peter Griffiths was elected in Smethwick on the slogan 'If you want a nigger for a neighbour, vote Labour'.[4] As the first black family moved into her street, young Brenda stood by the garden gate, horrified as neighbours shouted abuse at the incomers. As she called out to them to leave the newcomers alone, Brenda's mum hastily pulled her indoors, anxious to avoid further confrontation.

Timetable clashes at school prevented Brenda from taking her first 'A' level options of English, History and Biology, and she was obliged instead to study three sciences. Her results were disappointing, her studies distracted by boys, her part-time job at Boots the Chemist and exploring the wonders of Birmingham Library and Museum. Fortunately, a pass in Biology secured her a full-time job as a laboratory assistant, researching the causes of muscular dystrophy. Later, in the Genetics Department at Birmingham University, Brenda was responsible for the stocks of fruit flies, while studying for a Higher National Certificate (HNC) in microbiology.

Amongst her work colleagues was a PhD student called Edward Arthur, who was researching two different types of poppy. As their friendship developed, it became clear that wherever Edward went, Brenda would follow. When Edward was offered a research job at the recently opened John Innes Institute in Norwich, the couple married before moving south in July 1969, first to a rental house and six months later buying a home in the market town of Wymondham. Brenda's first job was at the Institute for Food Research, directly opposite John Innes, operating a state-of-the-art electron microscope. She enrolled at City College for the second year of her HNC, followed by a third year to bring her qualification up to degree level. Her final exam was in May 1972, just three weeks after giving birth to David. When he was nine months old, the family moved back into the city, buying a house close to the university, and their second son, Gareth, was born in May 1974.

Brenda was quickly involved with a group of university wives, who encouraged her to join a campaign for improved visiting rights for parents, working with the Norwich Association for the Welfare of Children in Hospital (NAWCH). With her boys loving to swim at the Spinney Youth and Community Centre, she was persuaded to join their committee, working with two chairmen, Ralph Roe and Dr Peter English, both Lord Mayors during the period 1977–79. Brenda quipped that it must be obligatory to be a Lord Mayor in order to be elected Chairman.[5] Gareth was about to join Larkman day nursery when Brenda was attracted to a job advertisement offering fifteen hours a week as a part-time community worker with the City Council. Her manager was Brian Horner, Team Leader in Community Development.

There followed a period of eleven tumultuous years, both professionally and personally. Brenda worked with many communities in the city, mainly dealing with issues faced by women of all ages. She established parent and toddler groups, junior youth clubs and recreation centres for senior citizens. In Birmingham, Ernest was facing redundancy for the second time. In 1983, aged sixty-four, he retired early and moved with his wife to Norwich to be closer to their daughter and grandsons. When Brenda was appointed as Activities Promoter for the Retired, Ernest and Irene offered their services. For many years, they led a popular arts and crafts group for older people, Irene teaching classes in lace making, embroidery and crochet, and Ernest sharing his love of painting. Ernest is remembered as a charismatic chairman of the Norwich Out and About Club, a social and friendship club for retired people that is still active today.

In 1986, with their marriage deteriorating, Brenda and Edward separated. Ernest and Irene were naturally upset and concerned for their grandsons, who were both students at Earlham School. When Irene complained of feeling unwell, the doctor suggested she might be suffering from stress. Not long afterwards, the diagnosis was changed. She had an inoperable cancer. Irene was stoic, and continued to lead her craft classes, even when confined to a wheelchair, carrying a supply of morphine to get her through the day. Irene died, aged sixty-two, in July 1988. Ernest remained outwardly strong, taking support from his many friends and continuing his art classes, and taking comfort in weekly fish and chip suppers with his adoring grandsons.

Brenda was now living with Brian Horner in the Aylsham Road. He encouraged her to become involved in his Labour Party activities, taking her to branch meetings and delivering leaflets together. This activity became a welcome distraction from her grief and part-time estrangement from her sons, who, for much of the week, lived with their father. In her professional life, Brenda joined the Board of Age Concern Norwich as a volunteer working with Chairman Joyce Morgan.[6] It was not long before a vacancy arose for a chief officer. Brenda was encouraged to apply, impressing Joyce and others with her strength of character. Brenda's brief was to develop and modernise the organisation, while attracting enough money to pay both her salary and those of her staff. This challenging position endured for the next seventeen years.

Within the first six months in her new role, Brenda rewrote the constitution and introduced computers. When her secretary retired, Brenda controversially replaced her with a man, causing consternation amongst the all-women team. She introduced both a befriending and a bathing service, while increasing the advice and information function. Four years later, the amended constitution dictated that Joyce had no choice but to stand down as chairman. She was reluctant and it was a delicate time, but with Joyce given the chance to mentor her successor, in 1994 she was finally content to walk away after more than ten years' service, convinced she was leaving her 'baby' in safe hands.

Age Concern Norwich operated out of the Advice Arcade, a City Council initiative established in the Old Lending Library on Gaol Hill. This one-stop shop housed a number of charitable organisations and community schemes, creating much interest from the outset with business leaders and politicians arriving to see it in action.[7] When financial pressures forced the City Council to close the Arcade, Age Concern Norwich moved to Boardman House on Princes Street, where Brenda rented out unoccupied rooms, including to high profile tenants such as Home Secretary and Labour MP for Norwich South Charles Clarke, and Ian Gibson, Labour MP for Norwich North. Of all the successful projects achieved under her leadership, Brenda is particularly proud of taking over the management of the Marion Road

Day Centre, specialising in caring for people with dementia – a well-respected project that continues to this day.

At a Christmas party in 2004, Council Leader Steve Morphew, a friend from the Labour Party, approached Brenda. He asked: 'We wondered if you'd like to be Sheriff?' Having established that this was not a joke and that the appointment would mark the sixtieth anniversary of Age Concern Norwich, Brenda accepted. She spent 'a bizarre year' fulfilling more than 250 civic engagements while continuing to work full time. 'I would go into work early and write my grant applications before the civic staff arrived with my robes and chain, then driving me to an event. Then it was back to the office and carry on.'[8] She was able to take advice from former civics amongst her board members, including Don Pratt and Jill Miller. Brian was supportive and her father was convinced that one day his daughter would be Lord Mayor of Norwich. But for that to happen, Brenda would need to become a city councillor.

Brenda and Brian had married in 1999, Brenda gaining two stepchildren, Matthew and Nancy. Despite this happiness, as her sixtieth birthday approached, Brenda became irrationally anxious about her future. Both her mother and grandmother had died in their early sixties. Was this to be her fate? Her solution was to retire from work and enjoy any time she might have left. Brian left his London job, taking on the role of Chief Executive of Voluntary Norfolk. With her children having successful careers and families, Brenda quickly became bored of shopping and lunches. She volunteered to be Chair of Norwich Carbon Reduction Trust and was employed as an agony aunt with BBC Radio Norfolk, thinking on her feet as listeners phoned in with their problems live on air! When her friends in the Labour Party suggested she might stand as a councillor in University Ward, she spoke with Brian. As ever, he was encouraging, and in May 2008, the name Brenda Arthur first appeared on a ballot paper.

She gained the seat from a Liberal Democrat, one of four wins for Labour that year, with a healthy majority of over 43 per cent. With the Green Party in the ascendant and Liberal Democrats losing ground, the City Council remained a minority administration. However, the Labour group held most seats and once again nominated a leader of the Council. Brenda was astonished when Steve Morphew suggested he put her name forward for a place on the Cabinet, almost unprecedented for a rookie councillor. With national government negotiations nearing completion on the question of unitary status for Norwich, city councillors were optimistically planning a new Cabinet position with responsibility for Older People, Health and Welfare. Brenda's experience made her an exact fit. She agreed, and was stunned to be immediately offered a second portfolio, this time for Housing.

There had been no Head of Housing for some time and over the following months Brenda and her team made it a priority to expose shortfalls in the system. With a government audit scheduled for the following February, it was important to listen to honest appraisals from outsiders. The results were disappointing. Before they had time to address the problems, the audit commission removed the Council's star rating, leaving Brenda and her colleagues exposed to damning press coverage and derision from political rivals. There was much hard work ahead, Brenda heading up a series of meetings with housing officers, tenants and councillors throughout the city. 'I used to say that officers were all going the extra mile, just in different directions. I just wanted to get everyone working together.' Gargantuan efforts along with her team meant the situation was turned around completely, with the equivalent of a two star rating for housing reinstated just two years later.

Believing that unitary status was imminent, Brenda was preparing to head up a new Adult Services Section. A general election was scheduled for May 2010, and sitting city councillors had their period of office extended for a further twelve months in order to maintain the status quo and ease the forthcoming transition. But the country returned a shock result, with no party having an overall majority; the eventual outcome was a Conservative and Liberal Democrat coalition under Prime Minister David Cameron. During the early autumn, the coalition shelved all plans for a unitary Norwich. Those councillors on an extended tenure were stood down with immediate effect, one of them being the Deputy Leader Brian Morrey, leaving a vacancy. Brenda unexpectedly found herself elevated to the number two position.

For six months she relished being at the heart of things, believing she could really make a difference. When Steve Morphew resigned his council seat in 2011, there was speculation as to who would take his place. Although Brenda was content to continue as Deputy, she was persuaded to put her name forward. On winning the vote, she became Leader of Norwich Council after only three years as an elected member. When attending meetings of the Local Government Association, she was not only shocked to discover she was one of only thirteen women leaders of district councils, but regularly stunned colleagues when answering the inevitable icebreaker, 'So, how long have you been a councillor?' On her watch, Norwich City Council built their first council houses for thirty years, the Olympic torch visited the city, and Norwich became UNESCO City of Literature. Hard work resulted in a number of national awards, including the coveted Most Improved Council of the Year and Best Council of the Year 2014, both welcome morale boosters for everyone working for the City Council.

However, in Brenda's personal life, the year 2013 brought further sadness. Ernest held on to his zest for life long after his wife died, finding a lady friend before losing her to cancer and relocating to a sheltered apartment in The Great Hospital,[9] where he ran an art class. His daughter idolised him: 'He was a very special man.' But in August, two weeks before his ninety-fourth birthday, Ernest died. Brenda was devastated. Early the following year, she faced a tough decision. With her seventieth birthday approaching in April 2017, she had already resolved not to stand for election in 2016. Norwich Labour Party rules state that a Leader must stand down after five years. Should she continue for a further, final year as Leader, a job she loved, or volunteer as Lord Mayor? Brian was due to retire, giving him time to be her consort and support. The grandchildren would love it. But it was when Brenda remembered her father's ambition for her that she knew what she had to do.

On 22 May, following the pomp of the Mayor-Making ceremony, the Lord Mayor and Sheriff stood together on City Hall steps, the first time the city had nominated two women for the roles in the same year. Beryl Blower, honoured for her charity work, was no stranger to civic tradition. Her husband Roy had been Lord Mayor in 2007, Beryl playing her part as Lady Mayoress. Brenda and Beryl were already acquainted, having met during election campaigns, Beryl being legendary for preparing running buffets at her home on polling days.

It was a year spent at full tilt, Brenda finding it particularly satisfying to share the joy with either Brian or with son David as consort. Her favourite event was the Lord Mayor's Procession. Despite a painful knee, Brenda walked the length of the route, drawing strength from Brian, her children and grandchildren, all gathered together to share her special day. The weather was perfect and the streets were lined with excited onlookers. The three older grandchildren, Dylan, Niamh and Evan, arrived with their parents David and Lizzy, with the two youngest, 4-year-old twins Adrienne and Grayson, travelling up with their parents Gareth and Imogen from their home in Surrey. The twins were dressed in pirate outfits, made for their recent birthday party. Brenda was amused when little Grayson said his grandma had the 'best pirate's' hat in the world'.

Another memorable day was in February 2016, when four former soldiers[10] from First Battalion Royal Norfolk Regiment, each involved in the D-Day landings on 6 June 1944, gathered with dignitaries, family and friends to receive the *Légion d'Honneur*, the highest decoration in France, from the Mayor of the French town of Blainville-sur-Orne. City Hall was decorated in the French colours, and as the visitors sang *La Marseillaise*, followed by a joint chorus of *Old Lang Syne*, Brenda was not the only one with a tear in her eye.

Later in June, at the City of Norwich School, Brenda joined an audience of children representing twenty-two schools from across Norfolk. At exactly 2.40 pm, the International Space Station would pass over the UK. As a young radio ham attempted to make contact, Brenda sat in the audience, the excitement palpable as, after a few agonising moments of static interference, a picture from space appeared on the giant screen, with celebrated British astronaut Tim Peake giving the youngsters a cheery wave. Over the next ten minutes, Tim answered a series of pointed questions. As the space station drifted out of range, everyone could not quite believe what had just happened.

Later in February, Brenda and Beryl joined the seventh annual 'Sleep Out' organised by the YMCA in Norwich, raising money for the city's homeless. A concrete area on Mousehold Common was equipped with a mountain of cardboard boxes and some fire pits. Unfortunately, knee problems meant Brenda was unable to lie down comfortably. Civic Attendant Gavin Thorpe delivered a camping chair and two cardboard boxes to wrap around her, adding to her layers of thermal vests, blankets and a woolly hat. By morning, after a cold night with very little sleep, the group roused to find a layer of frost and the wonderful smell of frying bacon.

Brenda's last day as Lord Mayor was also Gavin's last day as Attendant. He had been a loyal servant to the civics since 2006, looking after nine Lord Mayors and nine Sheriffs. With planned departmental changes and budget cuts afoot, it seemed to be a good time to call it a day. As he said goodbye, Gavin commented, 'I think we've seen the best of it, Brenda.' As she looked up from her final speech, the Council Chamber erupted into cheers and applause. It would be strange not going into City Hall every day. But Brenda remembered the words of her father, when speaking to him about an event in his younger life: 'That was in the past. I don't want to look back, I want to look forward.'

But first there was one more gown and hat waiting for Brenda. During the closing weeks as Lord Mayor she received an official looking letter from the University of East Anglia. She absorbed the contents, blinking in astonishment. Would she consider accepting an Honorary Doctorate of Civil Law at a graduation ceremony during the summer? With former Home Secretary Charles Clarke as her orator, and resplendent in purple academic gown and soft black beret, Brenda was delighted to accepted the scroll from Vice Chancellor David Richardson. During her address she confessed to having failed two 'A' levels, spending many years trying to compensate through day release study. But now, after fifty years, thanks to the city and the university, she finally had a degree.

Endnotes

1. Ernest Hird, 1921–2014, & Irene Siddaway, 1925–88.
2. A rare neurological disorder.
3. Ernest's father Joseph worked for Guest, Keen & Nettlefold, one of the world's largest iron and steel businesses.
4. http://www.telegraph.co.uk/news/obituaries/10479104/Peter-Griffiths-obituary.html
5. Brenda did later become Chairman of the Spinney Committee.
6. Joyce was Lord Mayor of Norwich 1975–76.
7. Visitors included Labour Leader John Smith and Conservative MP Eric Pickles.
8. Brenda Arthur, speaking in 2017.
9. The Great Hospital is a sheltered housing and care village in a building dating back to 1249, set in the Cathedral Quarter of Norwich.
10. Ken Mason, 97, from Norwich, David Johnson, 91, from Norwich, Bill Holden, 92, from Norwich, Victor Keech, 90, from Wymondham. James King's medal was awarded posthumously to his widow Brenda.

Brenda Arthur 2015–16

Further Highlights from her Mayoral Year

- Visiting Wensum Junior School to witness the work of civic charity Sistema, its aim to transform children's lives through participation in making music.

- Opening a branch of Quik Fit, a post office in the Cellar House Pub in Eaton, a bathroom at the Maid's Head Hotel and Bicycle Links, a bike hire centre and coffee bar in King Street, using a link cutter to ceremoniously cut through a bicycle chain.

- Singing *Jerusalem* in St Andrew's Hall, with more than 100 ladies, at the annual meeting of the Eastern Region Women's Institutes and finally realising that, in fact, the iconic hymn was not reserved for Brenda's former grammar school, where they had sung it every year on the last day of term.

- Presenting certificates to graduating students at City College, speaking about her three periods of study there.

- Meeting Terry Waite, former envoy to the Archbishop of Canterbury who, from 1987, was famously held in solitary confinement in Beirut by the radical group Hezbollah.

- Welcoming home troops from the Royal Anglian Regiment after active service in Afghanistan. Taking the salute as 250 servicemen and women marched past City Hall. Becoming emotional during her speech, and being rewarded with an enormous bear hug from four male soldiers.

- Watching the Dean of Norwich Cathedral, Jane Hedges, dancing with a Dalek during a science fair, with the cathedral full of exhibitions, scientists from the John Innes Centre, a mock-up volcano and a man blowing smoke rings.

- Meeting families at a special service at Norwich Cathedral organised by Survivors of Bereavement by Suicide. Feeling privileged, moved and inspired by their courage and willingness to share their stories.

- Attending the 100th anniversary service for Edith Cavell and watching with admiration, the four nurses standing like statues at each corner of her grave as heavy rain poured down, soaking their starched uniforms. Entering the railway carriage used to transport her body after her execution by a German firing squad.

- Joining the cast of *Peter Pan*, performing at the Theatre Royal, for the annual Pantomime Christmas Service at St Peter Mancroft. Taking granddaughter Naimh backstage after the show to meet actress and dancer Jennifer Ellison, star of *Dance Mums*, a reality television series, of which Naimh is a huge fan.

CHAPTER 17

Marion Frances Maxwell (1946–)

Lord Mayor of Norwich 2016–17

I have always been a socialist. My mother was a Conservative, I don't know why, and my dad was a socialist. I asked them once why they bothered going out to vote as they cancel each other out. My father said, 'You must vote, whatever way, you must always vote.' I loved the fact that he was very forgiving, especially as a policeman. I would say, 'But that man has been in prison …' and Dad would say, 'Yes, but he has served his time. He has to have a chance.'

(Marion Maxwell, speaking in 2016)

Following her inauguration as Lord Mayor of Norwich on 24 May 2016, on most days Marion Maxwell walked the short distance to work from her home in St Benedict's Street, through the market and up the steps into City Hall. She always made a point of talking with passers-by, shop assistants and market traders, her generous physique, flame-red hair and infectious laugh making her instantly recognisable. After her move to Norwich from Manchester in 1985, she fell in love with the city, never dreaming that one day she would be its First Citizen.

Marion Frances Clark was born in Manchester on 18 August 1946, her parents and grandparents hailing from Wales, Rotherham, London, Colchester, Kettering and the German region of Westphalia. Her two families merged in 1939 when Yorkshireman Stephen Clark from

Rotherham married Nellie Violet Mersy from Edmonton in Middlesex. Family legend tells how spirited teenage Nellie, while visiting London one summer's day in the late 1930s, was attracted to a young guardsman, standing tall in his Busby outside a Buckingham Palace sentry box. She cheekily proffered her ice cream cone to the soldier. Hardly moving a muscle, he whispered, 'Meet me here at six o'clock.' Nellie grinned, and the couple were married in Manchester a year later. During their engagement, Stephen left the Army, joined the Police Force and took a posting in Manchester, where Nellie joined him for their wedding. However, with the onset of war, Stephen was recalled to serve as a Military Policeman, and Nellie returned to Middlesex to live with her parents.

Marion's grandfathers had both seen active service in the Great War, and her father was no stranger to heroism, having fought in the notorious Battle of Monte Cassino in 1944 while responsible for a regiment of Ghurkha riflemen. Although the engagement was deemed an Allied victory, more than 4,000 Commonwealth servicemen were buried at the Cassino War Cemetery.[1] Stephen rarely spoke of it. He named his baby daughter after his hero John Wayne (real name Marion Morrison) and St Francis of Assisi, for reasons best known to himself. Marion wasn't their first child; Nellie had lost a son in 1940, following complications caused by her rhesus negative blood group, there being no medical facilities for changing the infant's blood.

Nellie gave birth to her second surviving son, Stephen William, in June 1952, his life saved by recent medical advancements. Nellie spoiled her boy, favouring him over Marion, who was a shy and serious child who quickly learnt to amuse herself. A promising student, Marion won a place at Urmston Grammar School, embarrassed by having to wear her father's cast-off shirts with the tails cut off, and envious of those arriving at school in expensive cars. Marion's ambition was to go to university, but on approaching her father, she received a hard lesson. 'Sorry lass, there is only enough money for one of you to go. You'll get married and have children, but your brother will have his family to support.'[2] This decision would haunt the family for many decades.

It was the early 'Swinging Sixties' in Manchester. Boys raced to learn the guitar, forming bands, hoping to make it big. When the young Beatles played at a local school fete, Marion and her friends avoided it, thinking it too downmarket for grammar school girls. And anyway, they preferred the Rolling Stones.

> We were a big gang of friends. There was a group on every week at various dance venues. The same tour of five or six groups would go to Liverpool one night and then Manchester the next. The Kinks were in residence at Belle Vue every Sunday.[3] It was fabulous. We once went to Jimmy Savile's Teen and Twenty Disco. I didn't like him.

With the post-war baby boomers now emerging as teenagers looking for work, jobs were scarce. Knowing that university was not an option and struggling with as yet unrecognised dyslexia, Marion left school a month before her fifteenth birthday, with a handful of GCEs. She received an offer from the Co-operative Insurance Company, where she once again faced discrimination against women. The company paid for men to train as underwriters, but women were not even offered the opportunity. Galvanised by this injustice, Marion joined the local Labour Party. Early in 1963, a client form relating to a convertible Triumph Herald passed across her desk. The driver's name was Richard Starkey. Marion instantly knew that this was Ringo Starr, the drummer from The Beatles. Excited, she considered copying down his home address, but being the daughter of a policeman she reluctantly rejected the idea.

Marion's next career move was to join the Civil Service, working as a temporary clerical assistant at the Ministry of Public Buildings and Works, based at Old Trafford, within sight of the football stadium. Between the two was a new tenpin bowling alley, where the young apprentices from Manchester United Football Club enjoyed a few frames when they weren't training. At lunchtimes the girls from the Ministry joined them, including 17-year-old Marion Clark. A dark-haired youth from Northern Ireland, about the same age as her, had been in Manchester for two years, yet was still homesick for Belfast. He was well mannered but painfully shy and didn't say much, but all the girls were wishing they could go out with him. Intrigued, Marion engaged him in light conversation. His name was George Best.

At twenty-one, Marion married a police officer; they were together for twelve years. She was in poor health for much of that time, undergoing surgery on two occasions. When she was twenty-nine, a mobile screening unit set up outside the office. Marion agreed to accompany a friend, not thinking to take the test herself. She was, however, persuaded to act as a patient for some students training on the equipment. The shock results showed Marion had an aggressive cancer of the uterus and ovaries. Four days later, she underwent a hysterectomy, remaining in intensive care for six weeks.

This life-changing event proved cataclysmic for Marion's marriage; the couple divorced amicably and went their own ways. In the mid-1980s, in need of a fresh start, Marion transferred to Norwich as an executive officer at Her Majesty's Stationery Office (HMSO), based in Sovereign House in Anglia Square. While still settling into the job, Marion found a breast lump. The tumour was tackled quickly, without the need for radical surgery, but nonetheless it had been a distressing time. She received invaluable friendship and support from her friends when, having recovered, she moved into a two-bedroomed flat in St Benedict's Street, a close community of independent stores and coffee bars.

With much in her life she wished to put behind her, Marion decided to officially change her surname. 'I had a friend in New York. Her stepson was called Michael Maxwell Katz, who tragically died of Aids. I thought I'd become Marion Maxwell in his honour.' For the next ten years Marion worked hard at HMSO including as a union representative, standing up for colleagues and challenging management when actions seemed unjust, and gaining a reputation as a force to be reckoned with. Marion loved discovering the distractions of the city and helping the local Labour activists, celebrating or commiserating with friends during elections. She enjoyed canvassing and speaking to people on the doorstep, but when first asked to stand as a councillor, she politely refused, citing her demanding full-time job.

On 20 December 1995, Marion was called to her father's bedside in Trafford Hospital. At 4.00 am, before slipping away, he made his peace, sorry for refusing to allow his daughter to follow her dream of studying at university. Now almost fifty and exhausted, Marion took early retirement from HMSO, receiving a generous lump sum. But before she could spend any of it, her mother also became ill. Marion returned to Manchester, nursing Nellie for two years. But with responsibilities back in Norwich, Marion returned home for a brief visit on 7 April 1999, disturbed by a persistent notion that her mother would die in the early hours, as her dad had done. At 8.00 am the following day, Marion received the news that Nellie had indeed passed away at exactly 4.00 am.

> Mum always wanted to see the Millennium, but she didn't quite make it. I think she probably wanted to be something special. She was a clever woman but never got the opportunities. She would have loved to have gone to grammar school. She came from a family of eight, where the love had to be shared out. She never kissed me goodbye or anything like that. I think that is why I am a very touchy feely person.

With no ties and a cash sum languishing in the bank, Marion booked a world trip. She and a friend visited New Zealand, Australia, Hong Kong, Bangkok, Singapore, Los Angeles, San Francisco and New York. 'When I found out I couldn't have children, I thought, "I am not going to waste my life." I made a list of places and I have been to them all.' Back in Norwich, with her windfall all but spent, Marion needed a job. She had previously worked for the Trades Union Congress (TUC) and was approached by UNISON to arrange training courses as part of an initiative called 'Return to Learn'. Marion became a field officer, travelling the Eastern Region, talking with people at their place of work – predominantly women working in hospitals – and encouraging them to study for a better future.

Contacts at the TUC suggested she apply for the post of Head of Trade Union Studies at City College Norwich. Marion was reticent; she was no academic and, anyway, she had a job working for UNISON. After weeks of gentle pressure, Marion gave in, especially when she discovered the office was just a short walk from her flat. Twenty-seven people applied. Despite having only two years before she could retire (again), the job was hers. She turned the department around, staying on for an additional year and walking away at sixty-one, preferring to give the opportunity to a younger person.

With more time on her hands, Marion became more involved in the local Labour Party, even agreeing to her name appearing on ballot papers in wards where Labour was unlikely to win. In 2011, Labour having lost the Norwich South seat to Liberal Democrat Simon Wright, a selection process was under way for a new Labour Prospective Parliamentary Candidate.[4] Marion volunteered to help one of the hopefuls, her friend David Rowntree, the drummer from the iconic nineties rock band Blur.[5] As they drove around the city, David taught her all the words to the Norwich City football song *On the Ball City*, while encouraging her to stand for a council seat, next time working to win. She was still unconvinced.

However, in 2012, her close friend Jenny Lay, a Labour councillor and former Lord Mayor, invited Marion to her home on Mousehold Heath. Jenny confided in Marion that her cancer had returned; she was tired and only had a short time to live. 'Marion, I want you to stand. I need to know that I'm leaving Crome Ward in safe hands.' Marion was torn. She had resisted this for such a long time. At nearly sixty-six, she still had other avenues to explore. Jenny persisted. Humbled and flattered, Marion agreed and stood for the City Council at the subsequent by-election and was elected with 61 per cent of the vote on 19 December 2012. 'The count was held in City Hall. When they announced the result I sat there thinking, "Good grief, I'm a councillor." I think I was in shock.'

Encouraged by Jenny's belief in her, Marion threw herself into the role, determined to make positive changes. She campaigned for social housing and traffic calming, and specialised in working with women's groups and holding surgeries for residents to vent their anger in her sympathetic ear. Amongst other positions, Marion was Vice Chair of Scrutiny Committee and sat on the Licensing Committee, enjoying the amusing tales told by the taxi drivers. Despite her dyslexia, she learnt to speed read in an effort to keep up with the inevitable mass of paperwork. As Chair of Mousehold Conservators, she loved walking on the Heath with the Rangers, monitoring the environment and enjoying a cup of coffee at a popular spot close to HMP Norwich's Café Britannia, staffed by low-risk prisoners.

After only three years as a city councillor, her colleagues suggested they nominate her as Lord Mayor for 2016–17. Once she recovered from the shock, she agreed, not believing it would come to anything. She was so convinced, in fact, that she booked herself a cruise, starting two days after Mayor-Making. But as her name was announced as the successful nominee at a special meeting, Marion was stunned. Deputy Leader Gail Harris looked concerned. 'Are you all right, Councillor? You look like you've been shot!'

It was the perfect early gift for her seventieth birthday in the August, and a welcome excuse to buy some new clothes. She took advice from former Lord Mayor Brenda Arthur as she slowly came to terms with this incredible opportunity. Marion, concerned about her dyslexia, was visibly nervous about her acceptance speech. 'I dare not write down my speeches because the words might fall off the page. I do it all from headings.' Her Sheriff was Richard Marks, the General Manager of John Lewis. As Marion and Richard stood on the steps for the formal photo call, they shared a sense of relief that the ceremony had passed without incident. Now the work could begin.

Or could it? Two days later, Marion left for her Baltic cruise, along with nephew Stephen, his partner Jacintha and her nephew Alexander. With a sense of mischievous pride, Marion noted her occupation in the captain's visitors book as 'Lord Mayor of Norwich', before joining his table as an honoured guest. On return to Norwich she embarked on her official engagements, accompanied each time by one of her three designated consorts, Deputy Leader Gail Harris, Councillor Mike Stonard and Alan Pawsey.

Marion chose a cancer support group as her civic charity, but this one was a little different. Her first opportunity to promote its work was at the all-male City Club, on the occasion of the annual Lord Mayor's Dinner. The evening did not start well, the chef having to prepare an individual dish for their honoured guest, the Lord Mayor being the only vegetarian in the room. Marion and consort Gail were also the only women, and as the time approached for her speech, Marion began to feel nervous, not sure of how it would be received. After a brief preamble, Marion announced, 'From now on guys, it's a load of balls, because I am here to talk about my civic charity "It's On The Ball", while encouraging you to examine yourselves for signs of testicular cancer.'[6] The 165 men in dinner suits laughed uproariously and before long she had their full attention.

Each summer, the Norwich Pride Parade brings a flash of colour and glamour to Norwich city centre, celebrating the lesbian, gay, bisexual and transgender (LGBT) community of Norwich and Norfolk. In 2016, the event was in its eighth year, with so many expected to participate that the route was switched to start outside City Hall, from where the iconic rainbow flags were displayed for the occasion. Wearing the red gown, matching perfectly with the images of the day, Marion gave a short address, concluding with: 'And finally, thank you for inviting me to this special day. I hope you enjoy yourselves and I'm very grateful that you asked a heterosexual old-age pensioner to kick off this march.' The laughter and joyful appreciation resounded around Market Square.

Marion's 'royal moment' came on 27 January, when Her Majesty the Queen and the Duke of Edinburgh arrived at the Sainsbury Centre for Visual Arts (SCVA), on the edge of the UEA Broad, to visit a new exhibition, 'Fiji: Art and Life in the Pacific'. The Queen had specifically asked to see this exhibition, particularly as amongst the 280 exhibits was a ceremonial whale tooth, the exact same one as was presented to her on their first visit to Fiji in 1953. Hundreds turned out to welcome the Royal party, including groups of excited schoolchildren wearing cardboard crowns and waving Union flags. Despite the cold, the male Fijian musicians wore the traditional dress, sporting impressive naked torsos. Everything went well but as the visit drew to a close, Marion received the instruction to escort the Queen to her car, a task of which the Lord Mayor had until that moment been blissfully unaware. 'The

Queen was so natural and delightful, I had no reason to feel nervous or overawed.'

Since 1757, the civic leaders of Norwich have worn the same chains of office, presented by wealthy dyer Matthew Goss. But for reasons of security and practicality, in the summer of 2016 the City Council commissioned new chains, the first for 250 years, designed in gold-plated sterling silver by local goldsmith Sonkai. Funded by the Freemen of Norwich, the chains were presented to Marion and Sheriff Richard Marks at City Hall in October. 'I like it. I was always petrified of wearing the other one. It's so heavy. I used to struggle getting it on and off and it ruins your hair!'[7]

On 23 May 2017, Marion's year as Lord Mayor came to a close. The ceremony to inaugurate Councillor David Fullman began, unusually, with a two-minute silence. The previous evening a terrorist attack had taken place at Manchester Arena, killing young concertgoers and their parents. Marion spent all night calling friends and family in her home city, checking they were safe and well. Despite being deeply shocked, she conducted the ceremony in a professional manner, earning respect and affection from those in the Chamber.

In her concluding speech Marion told of her most satisfying memory of her year. Norwich is proud of its long history of welcoming strangers to the city. On 8 July 2016, citizens were shocked by an overnight arson attack on 'The Village Shop', an eastern European food shop in Magdalen Street. Passers-by pitched in to help with the clean-up and a resident opened a JustGiving page to raise money for the Romanian family affected by this suspected hate crime. The Romanian Ambassador, Dan Mihalache, travelled to Norwich to show solidarity with the shop owners and to thank Norwich citizens for their compassion and support. Following his visit to Magdalen Street, Marion welcomed him to City Hall. On his way out, they walked along the corridor from the Lord Mayor's Parlour, the Ambassador admiring the civic portraits displayed on the walls. He turned to the Lord Mayor and said, 'You are wrong about Norwich being a Fine City.' During the momentary pause Marion's smile faltered, recovering swiftly as he added, 'It is *the* Finest.'

Endnotes

1. http://www.cwgc.org/find-a-cemetery
2. Marion Maxwell, speaking in 2016.
3. At a performance of The Kinks musical *Sunny Afternoon*, at the Theatre Royal, Norwich in April 2017, Marion confessed to a journalist that she had

been known to jump up on stage at a Kinks concert at Belle Vue, just to get a bit closer to her hero Ray Davies.

4.   Clive Lewis was selected as PPC, winning the Norwich South seat at the 2015 general election.

5.   On 5 May 2017, David Rowntree was elected as a Labour councillor on Norfolk County Council, holding University Ward with 59 per cent of the vote.

6.   A total of £22,843.83 was raised for the civic charity.

7.   The Mayor's magnificent gold chain, as presented to the city in 1757 by Matthew Goss, a wealthy dyer and Freeman, was in regular use for over three centuries until 2016, when the decision was made to replace it for everyday wear with a new chain of office. Similarly, the Sheriff's chain, a gift from Norwich sugar refiner Thomas Emerson in 1739, was also relegated to special occasions only. The Mayor's chain had always been heavy and uncomfortable to wear, its pins constantly tearing modern fabrics. Local goldsmith Sonkai won the design competition, creating two new gold-plated chains, the cost covered by the Freemen of Norwich and Norwich Town Close Estate Charity. The chains each have a total of eighteen motifs, representing aspects of the history of Norwich. These include Norwich Castle, printing, mustard, literature, Snap the Dragon, aviation, brewing and the boot and shoe industry.

Marion Francis Maxwell 2016–17

Further Highlights from her Mayoral Year

- Meeting Herbie, a beer-loving dray horse, outside City Hall, before being taken on the Woodfordes waggon to St John's RC Cathedral for the launch party for Norwich City of Ale 2016.

- Visiting the Plantation Garden to reopen the upper walkway above the garden's west bank.

- Enjoying the Lord Mayor's Celebration in July, including watching children on the giant water slide, launching the 5k road race from Agricultural Hall Plain, seeing the fireworks over the castle following a spectacular street procession including Snap the Dragon, samba dancers and Stormtroopers.

- Hosting her seventieth birthday tea party in the Lord Mayor's Parlour, where more than forty friends and colleagues packed the space to help celebrate. Meeting again with two former colleagues from HMSO nineteen years previously. Clearing up seventeen empty bottles of champagne.

- Sharing the podium outside City Hall during the Battle of Britain Parade, with RAF Marham Station Commander Group Captain Rich Davies, who calmed her nerves as they waited to walk through the double doors onto City Hall steps.

- Hosting the Christmas switch-on event with former shadow chancellor, *Strictly Come Dancing* star and Chairman of Norwich City Football Club, Ed Balls. Enjoying his performance of his Gangnam style dance before receiving a Christmas kiss!

- Attending Tobi's Ball in the Top of the Terrace at Norwich City Football Club, the major fundraiser for the civic charity It's On The Ball. Receiving an unexpected auction prize from David Rowntree, drummer from rock band Blur, in the form of a platinum disc, which alone raised £800 after vigorous bidding. Raising a total of £22,843 over her twelve months as Lord Mayor.

- Travelling to Koblenz, the twin city of Norwich, in March 2017, and receiving a warm welcome from Oberbürgermeister Professor Hofmann-Göttig before being shown around this beautiful city and eating a meal in the Altes Brauhaus, established in the historical Old Town in 1689.

- Attending the first International Nurses' Day Service at Norwich Cathedral.

- Opening the Eaton Dementia Friendly Community, an initiative set up by Councillor Caroline Ackroyd and her son Deputy Lord Mayor Councillor James Wright.

Bibliography & Sources

Most of the stories are taken directly from interviews, but the following archives, books, documents and websites have proved informative and inspirational.

Ancestry.co.uk

Archant Norfolk Archive.

Atkinson, R., *Norwich from a Stranger's Standpoint: An Address*, The Norwich Publicity Association, Norwich, 1931.

Banger, J., *Norwich at War*, Wensum Books, Norwich, 1974.

Chandler, M., *Historical Women of Norfolk*, Amberley Publishing, Stroud, 2016.

Colman, H.C., *Jeremiah James Colman: A Memoir*, privately printed at The Chiswick Press, 1905.

Colman's Detectives volunteer community, *Colman's Connections: The War Years, 1914–1918*, Norwich Heart, 2015.

East Anglian Film Archives at www.eafa.org.uk

Griffiths, E., & Smith, H., *'Buxom to the Mayor': A History of the Norwich Freemen and the Town Close Estate*, Centre of East Anglian Studies, 1987.

Goreham, G., *The Sheriff's Tale*, Crowes of Norwich, c.1986.

Guttsman, W.L., *The British Political Elite*, MacGibbon & Kee, London, 1968.

Hollis, P., *Ladies Elect: Women in English Local Government 1865–1914*, Clarendon Press, Oxford, 1987.

Holmes, F. & Holmes, M., *The Old Courts and Yards of Norwich: A Story of People, Poverty and Pride*, Norwich Heritage Projects, 2015.

Holt, T. & Holt, V., *The Biography of Captain Bruce Bairnsfather*, Pen & Sword Military, Barnsley, reprinted 2014.

Ludham Community Archive at http://www.ludhamarchive.org.uk

Meeres, F., *Dorothy Jewson Suffragette and Socialist*, Poppyland Publishing, Cromer, 2014.

Norfolk Heritage Centre.

Norfolk Record Office.

Norfolk Wherry Trust.

Norwich Heart at www.heritagecity.org

Palgrave-Moore, P., *The Mayors and Lord Mayors of Norwich*, Elvery Dowers, 1978.

Sanderson, M., *The History of the University of East Anglia Norwich*, Hambledon & London, London, 2002.

Thorpe History Group Archive as held at Thorpe St Andrew Town Council.

Index